INNOVATION DISTRICTS
A TOOLKIT FOR URBAN LEADERS

ARNAULT MORISSON

Copyright © 2015 by Arnault Morisson

First Printing, 2015

ISBN-13: 978-1515340621

ISBN-10: 1515340627

www.innovating-cities.com

"19th century was a century of empires. The 20th century was a century of nation states. The 21st century will be a century of cities."

Wellington E. Webb, former mayor of Denver in office 1991-2003.

TABLE OF CONTENTS

INTRODUCTION

In 1981, Sherwin Rosen published an article titled "the Economics of Superstars" in which she suggested that, "the phenomenon of Superstars, wherein relatively small numbers of people earn enormous amounts of money and dominate the activities in which they engage, seems to be increasingly important in the modern world." Rosen demonstrates that a marginal difference in luck and talent results in a tremendous disparity of earnings between individuals. I believe that the revolutionary nature of the Information and Communication Technologies (ICT), namely the Internet, has magnified disparities to various extents in every aspect of human life. The repercussions of ICT have not spared cities, and we are witnessing the rise of superstar cities such as Austin, New York, San Francisco, London, and Hong Kong, to name just a handful. In this new economic paradigm, urban leaders can use innovation districts as the impetus for their cities to attain or retain their superstar status.

Innovation districts are being implemented to spark urban regeneration in cities as diverse as Barcelona (Spain), Boston (Massachusetts), Chattanooga (Tennessee), Detroit (Michigan), Medellin (Colombia), and Montréal (Canada). Despite their prevalence, however, little is known about the concept of innovation districts. It seems like every city in the United States is working towards having its own version of an innovation district; however, if one looks beyond the rebranding efforts, it becomes clear that most have what are innovation districts in name only.

This book has the ambition to clearly define what an innovation district is, as well as provide readers with a rigorous framework to design their own. It is possible for cities to become more innovative and thus more competitive, so long as urban leaders implement the right policies at the right time. As Steve Jobs emphasized when describing his tremendous success in the documentary, Triumph of the Nerds, "I feel incredibly lucky to be at exactly the right place in Silicon Valley, at exactly the right time historically where this invention (the computer) has taken form." Innovation districts create the artificial reef to nurture an innovative ecosystem that makes radical innovations such as Apple Computer Inc. possible. This book will formulate its own artificial reef recipe for designing innovation districts that accelerate cities' innovative capacity.

We live in a period of transition—from mass-production to mass-specialization, from stable to flexible employment, from stable to flexible family structures, from creative destruction to disruptive technologies. Disruptive means that a new technology is destroying more jobs than it is creating. The transition means increased competition in the two most important matters of modern human lives: dating and working. The transition is being facilitated by the supreme value of individual freedom (the world order would have collapsed into anarchy without the parallel emergence of individual freedom, but that is a subject for another book).

In this transition, cities are more relevant today than ever before. Globalization and the revolutionary nature of information and communication technologies (ICT) have strengthened the economic power of a number of global cities as hubs of innovation and wealth creation. While the economic power of countries has declined, cities are re-emerging as key players of the new economic order.

It doesn't mean, however, that every city is gaining from the transition. What is emerging is a concentration of power to key urban centers. A steady decline awaits a large majority of cities. The distinctive feature of successful cities is now, and will be even more so in the future, their innovative capacities. Innovation lies at the heart of political debate in developed countries, to the extent that for policymakers a sustained competitiveness can only arise through the development of knowledge-intensive activities. Competition between cities will become stronger as technology advances. Although competition between cities is not as desirable as for companies since it will increase the gap between thriving and declining cities and thus creating social distress. The upcoming fierce competition between cities offers opportunities for pioneer cities to develop innovative policies and strategies that will allow them to thrive and prosper.

Cities are organic phenomena that have to adapt to new economic and technological paradigms in order to flourish. A new technology has a strong influence on urban planning. Indeed, the functionalist cities (e.g. Los Angeles (USA), Brasilia (Brazil)…) were built around the automobile, while the smart cities of today are built around the ICT (e.g. Songdo (South Korea)). From the 1970s to the 1990s, local and regional governments were building technology parks outside cities, such as Sophia-Antipolis in France or the Research Triangle Park in North Carolina. The strategy of those initiatives was to create a scientific cluster and to recreate the excitement of the city, and in the case of Sophia-Antipolis, a *Quartier Latin*, far from the structural chaos and inefficiencies of cities.

In the beginning of the 21st century, the rise of the global economy and the revolutionary nature of ICT caused innovation to flow back to urban areas. The highly localized nature of knowledge-intensive activities and a large number of converging factors help to explain the renewal of urban areas and the relative decline of the suburbs. As Peter Hall (1988) pointed out, 20th century urban planning "represents a reaction to the evils of the nineteenth-century city." 21st century urban planning with its deep urban locus is thus a reaction of the evils of the 20th century, which included congestion, accidents, urban sprawl, pollution, and public fiscal costs. This book will explore the transformations taking place at the urban level.

Barcelona is and has always been a leader in urban experimentation. Scholars have coined the term "Barcelona model" to describe the city's avant-gardism with respect to urban innovation. Following this tradition, Barcelona is the first city in the world to have developed an innovation district—also known as 22@ Barcelona—which has become one of the iconic urban strategies being replicated around the world. Boston (USA), Medellin (Colombia), and

Montréal (Canada) have implemented innovation districts modeled on 22@ Barcelona. Among those newly formed innovation districts, Boston's Innovation District, which launched in 2010, is at an advanced stage.

The concept of innovation districts is the response to new productive conditions emerging from globalization and advances in ICT. It is the byproduct of theories in innovation and a convergence of social and technological forces. Chapter 1 explores the new paradigm that makes cities so relevant in the knowledge economy. Chapter 2 deals with the shift in preference from suburbia to city centers. Chapter 3 aims to understand why the development of innovation districts, rather than technology parks, is the most efficient strategy for boosting a city's economic growth. Chapter 4 defines innovation districts. Chapter 5 introduces the recipe for building an innovation district. Chapter 6 looks at the prerequisites for making an innovation district a successful strategy for your city. Finally, three case studies of successful and established innovation districts in Barcelona, Boston, and Singapore provide proven models that can be replicated in your city. This book is dedicated to urban leaders and urbanites with a strong desire to make their cities more innovative and more interesting.

1

THE INNOVATIVE PARADIGM

In the knowledge economy, cities are re-emerging as central economic and political actors. Two converging and interdependent factors explain the resurgence of cities – globalization and knowledge. Globalization is forcing countries to adopt standards and is limiting their sovereignty. The increasing importance of knowledge in economic production has reinforced the stickiness of location. The highly localized nature of knowledge-intensive activities will force cities to adopt strategies in favor of innovation in order to remain competitive.

Policymakers and academic scholars have taken a renewed interest in urban matters. Cities compete just as nations and regions do, and they compete with one another. There is, however, an increased emphasis on competition between cities as the competition between countries declined. The competition between cities has been fostered by structural changes like globalization and the advent of new technologies, which "are taking place outside of the cities and are primarily beyond their control" (Braun & van Winden, 2014). Transformations that are happening at the global, pluri-national, and national scales are strengthening the economic and political power of cities. At the global scale, new constituted networks of economic activity - such as finance, trade, foreign direct investments, international joint ventures, are beginning to be regulated by a system of international contractual regimes, understandings, and organizations. At the pluri-national scale, newly formed multinational trading blocs and free-trade areas—such the EU, NAFTA, ASEAN, APEC, CARICOM, and MERCOSUR—are limiting the power of the sovereign nation state, and its economic and political independence. At the national scale, the dismantlement of the welfare state, neoliberal reforms, processes of decentralization, and structural labor-reforms imply that countries are converging on an economic and policy standard.

As a consequence of these transformations, political and economic power is shifting from the national to the local level. Cities are re-emerging as powerful economic and political actors. The competitiveness of cities is becoming a priority for policymakers. The urban realm is increasingly seen as a laboratory for policy experimentation.

FROM MASS-PRODUCTION TO KNOWLEDGE-INTENSIVE

Capitalism is undergoing a transformation from mass-production to knowledge-intensive. The transformation of the modes of production from Fordism to Post-Fordism implies a restructuring at the urban level. Fordism entails that the principal source of economic value is physical labor; Post-Fordism, however, requires the ability to harness workers' intelligence, creativity, and knowledge. In the new economy, it is not physical labor, but human creative capabilities that generate value (Florida & Kenney, 1993). Successful cities are the ones that are adapting best to this paradigm-shift.

This paradigm-shift from mass production to knowledge-intensive, which was initiated by technological innovations, has deeply modified the socio-economic urban structures. The shift to the knowledge economy is removing the barriers that once separated innovation from production—the laboratory from the factory—and is reshaping the whole organization of production (Florida & Kenney, 1993).

Metropolitan regions and urban centers are the outcome of economic and political forces. The prevailing economic structure and dominant technology of the time shapes how cities are designed, what economic activities are privileged, and how cities aim to achieve prosperity. The role of cities in national economies has changed significantly in the past few decades because of globalization and other structural adjustments. Understanding these transformations is critical for successful regional economic analysis and development planning. In the 1970s, the oil crisis, the global economy, the loosening of trade barriers, the emergence of a new form of economic production and management, the focus on competitiveness and productivity, and the advent of new technologies—namely information and communication technologies—set the world on the path towards the information economy in which knowledge-based industries are the main engines of economic prosperity. As a result, the economic gravity has moved from industrial cities such as Detroit (United States) or the Ruhr (Germany), to innovative and entrepreneurial cities and regions such as Bangalore (India), the Silicon Valley (United

States), Tel Aviv (Israel), and Route 128 (United States).

Urban leaders and policy-makers need to understand the implications of the paradigm shifts that are occurring in economic policy, and they need to develop strategies to effectively compete in the knowledge economy. The ability of a metropolitan area to adopt strategic policies will determine its future competitiveness. Economic policies and political dogmas shape the way regional and local areas think and plan for the future. At the city level, however, some regional economic development policies still remain embedded in the paradigms of the 1970s, such as giving tax breaks and economic incentives to companies (Stimson, Stough, & Roberts, 2006).

At the local and regional level, the policy lens has moved from the model of Hecksher-Ohlin's comparative advantage to Michael Porter's competitive advantage, and it has, more recently, progressed to collaborative advantage (Stimson et al., 2006). The shift from Hecksher-Ohlin's comparative advantage to Michael Porter's competitive advantage is exemplified by the shift from the smokestack-chasing strategy of offering fiscal and economic incentives, to the nurturing of innovation ecosystems such as innovation districts. The smokestack-chasing strategy adopted by cities resembled the cost leadership approach developed by Michael Porter, and therefore was a zero-sum game. Today, a number of cities within developed countries are adopting a differentiation strategy, appealing to companies to relocate because of genuine interests to do so, such as access to talented, "creative" professionals, institutional supports, quality of life, an overall improved innovative capacity, and so on. Innovation districts such as 22@ Barcelona, Boston's Innovation District, and one-north Singapore, among many others, are adopting this differentiation strategy. The cities that are implementing innovation districts aim to attract companies and individuals not through fiscal and economic incentives, but by providing what innovative companies and young professionals want.

The differentiation strategy adopted by some cities around the world aims to attract knowledge-intensive activities since they are perceived by urban leaders as tools to reorganize the economy towards a more intensive use of the urban economic fabric. The productive focus on knowledge-intensive activities has three main benefits for a city. First, knowledge-intensive activities provide a means for the city to remain competitive and boost productivity. Second, knowledge-intensive activities create high-quality jobs and produce a positive multiplier effect for the city. Third, knowledge-intensive activities are highly localized and provide a sustained economic advantage for the city.

Urban leaders have promoted the development of knowledge-intensive activities as a tool for urban areas to remain competitive and boost productivity. The paradigm-shift from labor-intensive to knowledge-intensive has pushed urban areas to reorganize their productive apparatus. The loss of the traditional comparative advantage in developed economies due to globalization and the ICT revolution has resulted in rising unemployment rates and increased outsourcing to lower-cost locations in Central Europe, Latin America, and Asia (especially

China). This in turn has led governments to promote the knowledge-based economy as a kind of shock therapy to renew economic growth and productivity. The strategy involves shifting economic activity away from traditional industries, in which high-cost countries have lost their comparative advantages, and towards the knowledge-based industries, in which the comparative advantage is compatible with both high wages and high levels of employment. Indeed, national competitiveness is primarily achieved through knowledge-based industries, within which a nation needs to specialize to obtain a world-class standard of living for its citizens.

Knowledge-intensive activities create high-quality jobs and are, for urban policy makers, the panacea to higher quality of life and productivity. When comparing the Silicon Valley to the U.S. average, between 1992 and 1996, the Silicon Valley has created 15% more jobs, and wages have increased by 50% (Audretsch & Thurik, 1999). For Enrico Moretti (2012), an innovation job, from a city's point of view, is more than a job because it produces a multiplier effect. Indeed, the indirect effects on the local economy are much larger than the direct effects. Moretti's research (2012), based on an analysis of 11 million American workers in 320 metropolitan areas, showed that for each knowledge-intensive job created in a metropolitan area, five additional local jobs are created outside of the knowledge-intensive activities in the long run. These five jobs benefit a diverse set of workers. Two of the jobs created by the multiplier effect are professional jobs, such as those of doctors or lawyers, while the other three benefit workers in nonprofessional occupations such as waiters or store clerks (Moretti, 2012). All parts of the trade sector have a multiplier effect, but innovation has the largest. Moretti's analysis indicates that attracting one job in traditional manufacturing generates 1.6 additional local service jobs—less than one third of the corresponding figure for high-tech jobs (Moretti, 2012).

Knowledge activities are highly localized and depend on many factors, such as innovative milieu, research and development (R&D) facilities, and knowledge workers (who are not easily outsourced). For urban policy makers, promoting knowledge-intensive activities secures a sustained competitive advantage in the long run. The emergence of geographic regions where both wages and employment are expanding, despite the great recession, such as the Silicon Valley in California, the Research Triangle in North Carolina, and Cambridge in the United Kingdom, are examples of such successful knowledge-intensive regions in the midst of globalization and a world dominated by ICT. Although the ICT revolution and globalization make locations irrelevant for many activities, location is essential for knowledge-intensive activities. Indeed, the difference between the two lies in the distinction between knowledge and information. Information consists of facts, which can be transmitted around the world without cost. Companies that are mostly made of information can easily be outsourced. By contrast, knowledge, especially tacit knowledge, consists of ideas that are subjective, uncertain, and difficult to explicitly write down and thus even more difficult to outsource. Tacit knowledge arises as a result of face-to-face contact and exchange that can only take place at the level of the city and the district. Indeed, as passionately demonstrated by Jane Jacobs (1961), creative ideas, tacit knowledge, and innovation are sometimes the consequences of chance meetings and serendipitous encounters. Moreover, the productivity of knowledge-intensive activities is not subject to diminishing returns, but to increasing returns; it becomes, on average, cheaper and cheaper to generate additional increments of knowledge. This idea of increasing returns is easy to visualize with companies like Facebook or Twitter for instance, where an additional user does not cost anything to the company, the sunk cost is limited, and growth is unlimited. Innovation, as a result, can be a source of unlimited growth, and it can be the key to a higher standard of living, sustained growth, and high employment rates in some urban areas.

The competition among cities to attract knowledge-intensive activities and build innovative ecosystems that favor the rise of innovative activities is intensifying due to how innovation is being redistributed. As Jaron Lanier demonstrated in *"Who Owns the Future?"* the way the economic surplus of innovation is being redistributed creates a negative-sum game, more jobs are being destroyed than created. The ICT revolution has destroyed more jobs in music and media than it has created in those same industries. For Lanier, if the system doesn't change (how the economic surplus of innovations is redistributed), the drastic changes that happened to the music and media will happen to most industries. Future innovations such as self-driving cars, MOOCs, 3D printers, and robots will cause mass-unemployment. Wealth inequalities will drastically rise between the innovators (and technologies' owners) and the adopters of new technologies. Competition and strategies to attract, retain, and create knowledge-intensive activities will be the crucial determinants of success for cities and a simple matter of survival.

Hob Lipson is a renowned technologist and professor who aims to design machines that can design other machines. Lipson's interests include evolutionary robotics, artificial intelligence, and artificial life. Even forefront technology hobbyists like Lipson are preoccupied by the destructive power of technology when he declares: "Now the evidence is that technology is destroying jobs and indeed creating new and better ones but also fewer ones. It is something we as technologists need to start thinking about" (Rotman, 2015). Job polarization and the hollowing out of the middle class in the most economically advanced countries of the world are realities. This postulate was proposed by Jeremy Rifkin (1995) in the *end of work*. Although the end of work is unlikely in the foreseeable future, a redefinition of the concept of work is likely to emerge. Work has become more precarious, flexible, entrepreneurial, and unequal, especially for the young generations, who prefer to become YouTubers or Bloggers rather than doing Excel spreadsheets for minimum wage in a cubicle from 9am to 5pm. Jeremy Rifkin (1995) points out that society risks becoming chaotic if policymakers do not address the problems of unemployment and underemployment. Technology is the poison and the remedy. When the surplus it creates is wrongly distributed, technology has the potential to lead us into another dark age.

2

FROM SUBURBIA TO URBAN DELIGHT

In the most advanced world economies, a strong and lasting trend for urban living is re-emerging. Urban living is re-associated with status, sophistication, open-mindedness, and the undeniable hip factor. TV screenwriters have identified this trend of suburban vs urban living, Desperate Housewives vs Sex and the City, or Breaking Bad vs Mad Men. In Breaking Bad, the main character, Walter White, is so tired of his dull suburban lifestyle in Albuquerque, New Mexico, that he starts producing crystal meth. Although quite extreme, Breaking Bad is, as are many pop culture productions, an analogy of the dichotomy between the suburban and urban classes. The suburban class lives a dull but prosperous life while the urban class lives a fun but careless life. The trend to favor urban living is going to grow due to a large set of factors that emerge not only from a top-down approach to promote sustainability and a better use of urban amenities, but also from a deep-changing pattern in lifestyle and consumption. Indeed, the rise of the experience economy, evolving family structures, disinterest in the automobile, and the ambiguous line between work and leisure all contribute to make living in cities a fun and transformative experience.

Urban planners can be separated into two groups: decentrists, such as Le Corbusier and Frank Llyod Wright, who favor urban sprawl to limit the problems of industrial cities; and centrists such as Jane Jacobs and Léon Krier, who favor high density cities and decry urban sprawl (Breheny, 1996). In developed countries, there is a strong trend toward centrist as those countries already have experienced decentrist planning (and its dreadful consequences). As Hall (1988) pointed out, 20th century urban planning "represents a reaction to the evils of the 19th century city." 21th century urban planning is, thus, a reaction to the evils of the 20th century. The policies that determine the nature of city planning cannot be separated from politics, because building cities is an expression of politics. In the 20th century, urban planners aspired to create well-organized and sane communities away from the disease and congestion of industrial towns. Le Corbusier, 1887-1965, a Swiss born architect, wanted to create machine-like mass-produced cities for the mass-production age, "the results (of Le Corbusier's ideas) were at best questionable, at worst catastrophic" (Hall, 1988). In the 21th century, urban planners aspire to shape sustainable, efficient, and creative communities for the knowledge economy.

In the late 19th century, Ebenezer Howard introduced the concept of "Garden Cities." He came to the conclusion that the growth of cities was uncontrollable. While the countryside was underutilized, the growing urban population led to congestion and system overload. Garden cities were a new pattern of city development to break down the widening gap between the countryside, with its depleted economic and social facilities, and the city, with its equally depleted biological and natural characteristics (Mumford, 1961). In 1904, the first garden city was built near London in Letchworth (Mumford, 1961).

Frank Llyod Wright and Le Corbusier, the two most influential architects and urban planners of the 20th century, were deeply influenced by the ideas of Ebenezer Howard (Mumford, 1961). Le Corbusier was an Arch-centrist and Frank Llyod Wright was a decentrist. Le Corbusier's Ville Radieuse leads to zoning and Llyod Wright's Broadacres City was the catalyst model for urban sprawl (Burton, Jenks, & Williams, 2003). For Le Corbusier, cities had to adapt to modern modes of transportation and automation, such as the automobile and elevator. For Le Corbusier (1946), the rational occupation of a territory could enable the population to become more productive and reduce work hours by half. In order to achieve the rational occupation of a territory, vertical gardens cities had to replace garden cities (Le Corbusier, 1946). The Athens charter, also called the functionalist planning, was largely influenced by Le Corbusier and stated that modern urbanism should reflect four fundamental functions: living, working, recreation, and circulation. People should be able to fulfill their potential within a context where sun, space, and greenery predominated (Le Corbusier, 1946). Le Corbusier's planning concepts were largely replicated by the automobile and oil lobbies. During the 1939 World's Fair in New York, the automobile and oil lobbies presented a modern city named Futurama. The dream city envisioned by the lobbies was identical to Le Corbusier's Radiant City

(Montgomery, 2013). The model of individual transportation and zoning are exemplified in Brasilia (Brazil), planned by Lúcio Costa and Oscar Niemeyer and inspired by the Radiant City, or in Chandigarh, a city in India planned by Le Corbusier.

The de-concentration promoted by Le Corbusier and Frank Llyod Wright led to zoning, suburban sprawl, and verticality, which have a negative impact on efficiency by generating externalities such as spillover costs, congestion, pollution, accidents, and public fiscal costs. Moreover, 20th century urban planning has affected social life, added in time-loss complexity, and reduced diversity. The functionalist replacement of vibrant streets by mono-function shopping malls, gated communities, schools, and hospitals isolated and separated from each other, convert cities into closed systems. Jane Jacobs (1961) was one of the first urban theorists to oppose the single-use standard of urban planning. Jane Jacobs advocated for diversity and mixed-use zoning. Living in New York City, she experienced the Robert Moses' urban renewal plan that replaced well-functioning neighborhoods with immense towers that were isolated from the streets that surrounded them.

Besides having totally remodeled cities, the work of Le Corbusier and Frank Llyod has also served to create a counter movement of urban romanticists, led by Jane Jacobs, and New Town Planning theorists, led by Léon Krier. Those urban romanticists began to flow back to inner cities in the late 1960s, moving to decaying manufacturing areas such as New York City's Soho in lower Manhattan. The pioneer spirit to re-conquer relinquished districts was first led by artists and the creative industry before becoming a popular way of life for the creative class.

For Jane Jacobs, the city is a social entity, and urban planning should reflect this fact. Urban planning should enable neighborhoods to be as diverse as possible, be walkable, be interesting, and foster social life. Jacobs (1961) believes in simple terms that "if a city's streets look interesting, the city looks interesting; if they look dull, the city looks dull." For her, four conditions are necessary to generate diversity in a neighborhood. First, the district must serve more than one primary function—preferably more than two. This ensures the continuous presence of people at any time of day or night, which in turn makes streets safer. Second, street blocks must be short in order to enable frequent turns. Third, the district must have a good balance of old and new buildings, so that the economic and social structures vary. Fourth, the district should be diverse and have a high population density (Jacobs, 1961). Urban diversity is self-perpetuating, and since small businesses are attracted to diversity, it will generate economic benefits for the city (Jacobs, 1961). For Jacobs (1969), knowledge spillovers are related to the diversity of industries in an area because diverse urban environments, in which people with different backgrounds and interests live, stimulate innovation. Urban planning should adopt continual, gradual, complex and subtle change, rather than radical change (Jacobs, 1961). For Jacobs (1961), "dull inert cities are facing an inexorable decline;" however, "lively, diverse, and intense cities contain the seeds of their own regeneration."

Léon Krier is another opponent of functionalist urban planning. For him, as for Jane Jacobs, while the idea of zoning is a powerful one because of "its rational and orderly nature," the concentration in sterile, regulated zones of housing, culture, and production means the destruction of the essence and diversity of the urban fabric (Krier, 1978). The model of the European city with the traditional urban block, street pattern, and mixed-uses should be reintegrated in urban planning (Krier, 1984). For Krier, the city's social, economic, and cultural complexities necessarily depend on its density and physical and structural complexity (Krier, 1984). Urban quarters are at the center of urban planning and should reflect the complexity of a city. Each quarter must have its own center, periphery, and limit, and each quarter must be a city within a city (Krier, 1977). In order to mirror the dimensions of pre-industrial cities, the quarter must integrate all daily functions of urban life (living, working, and leisure) within a territory limited to 35 hectares in surface area, and with a population of no more than 15,000 inhabitants (Krier, 1977).

Urban planning is a manifestation of political and social trends. The centrists' view is promoted not only by the political elite, but also is adopted by individuals due to shifting preferences. There is a transition from suburban to urban preferences among a large and increasing percentage of the population. The transition is facilitated by the rise of the experience economy, changing demographics and family structures, the decline of the automobile, and shifting work patterns.

Pine and Gilmore (1998) reveal the shift from consumption of material goods to the consumption of experiences. While the consumption of material goods was a suburban phenomenon, the consumption of experiences is an urban phenomenon. The consumption of experiences is facilitated in cities, and the shift toward the experience economy implies that consumers participate in the new consumption paradigm. The sharing economy (e.g., Airbnb, eBay, BlaBlaCar, Zipcar…), interactive shopping experiences (e.g., Whole Foods, farmers' markets, and "third places" such as third-wave coffee houses…), and cultural and sportive events (e.g., concerts, museums, biking…) are all manifestations of the new experience economy, where people become active rather than passive consumers. The inner city facilitates the experience economy to the extent that experiences become more accessible in cities than in the suburbs. The urban core generates sufficient diversity for an organic and indigenous street-level culture in which residents build a sense of community and trust among each other. Connectedness and proximity to diverse and numerous amenities make city-living the best way to participate in the experience economy.

In *Going Solo*, Eric Klinenberg (2011) demonstrates that the renewed interest in living downtown is closely related to changing demographics and family structures. Retiring baby-boomers, urban millennials, single parents, and one-person dwellings all contribute to a renewed urban appeal. Modern cities, especially with respect to the suburbs, were designed for nuclear families or families in which the mother stays at home while the father works elsewhere (Klinenberg, 2012). Changes in family structure have created the need to redesign cities and their suburbs to accommodate single parents and singleton living. Massive demographic shifts indicate that these pro-urban segments are predominating. In Manhattan, nearly half of all residences are one-person dwellings (Klinenberg, 2012).

Retiring baby boomers want to live in the urban core so as to remain independent for a longer time than if they were living in the suburbs, while urban millennials wish to live in the core to engage in more activities, for instance dating, while maximizing the number of positive new experiences. Single parents want to live in the urban core to live a relatively short distance from where they work and not have to commute for hours. Both young workers and retiring baby boomers are actively seeking to live in densely packed, mixed-use communities where residences, shops, schools, parks, and other amenities exist close to one another (Wieckowski, 2010). Living in the inner city is also the natural choice for bachelor living. For any man who has lived the bachelor lifestyle knows that proper logistics as well as some game and a large suitable pool of potential mates are essential for success when dating. You want to have as many cool venues, restaurants, and bars as close to your pad as possible while maximizing the potential number of Tinder matches. In contrast, as a single woman, you want to live in the same area of the city in which you go out, so that if the date goes badly, at least you can quickly return home for a nice cup of hot chocolate.

The percentage of millennials—people born between 1980 and 2000—driving, possessing a driver's license, or owning a car, is significantly lower than that of the previous generation (Neff, 2010). Not owning a car is seen by many millennials as a path to greater flexibility, choice, and personal autonomy. Online applications (Uber), car-pooling (BlaBlaCar), and short time car renting (ZipCar) contribute to make owning a car a luxury rather than a necessity. Walking or biking is increasingly becoming a way of life. City residents, especially millennials, prefer communities with street life (Speck, 2013). For Speck, urban designers should promote walkability, and sidewalks must satisfy four conditions: they must be useful, safe, comfortable, and interesting (Speck, 2013). People are paying three times as much per square foot for apartments in walkable neighborhoods as compared to suburban homes, and the demand for walkable urban housing far outpaces the supply (Speck, 2013). Moreover, rising oil prices, longer commutes, and congestion are further causing people to seek out more central locations. The decline of the automobile is partly a reaction to the disadvantages of suburban living. Indeed, people living in the suburbs suffer higher rates of obesity, psychological problems, and cardiovascular diseases than people living in the urban core (Speck, 2013). Research by behavioral economist Daniel Kahneman et al. (2004) showed that, out of a number of daily activities, commuting has the most negative effect on people's moods (sex has the most positive effect on people's mood).

The promotion of entrepreneurship, continuous learning, the increasing number of freelancers, the rise of the creative class, and the necessity of networking and flexibility are some of the factors blurring the frontier between work and personal life. Indeed, after-work happy hours for socializing and networking, business meetings in informal locations, start-up weekends, business events, coffee places where venture capitalists and start-ups meet, and casual encounters where advice is exchanged are some of the reasons why young creative professionals choose to live and work in urban centers. Digital companies are using urban locations as a recruiting tool to attract top talent: examples include Zappos in downtown Las Vegas, LinkedIn in downtown San Francisco, and the start-ups locating in the Silicon Alley and Manhattan. Yelp and Zynga have also actively used urbanism as a recruiting tool. In the new economy, the line between leisure and work is blurred, as the urban headquarters of these companies, where ping-pong tables and meeting rooms coexist, illustrates. Jacobs (1961) emphasized the important role that urban planning plays in fostering entrepreneurship. Indeed, according to Jacobs (1961), diversity breeds diversity, and is the foundation for creative endeavors and entrepreneurship.

In the *Hacker Ethic*, Himanen (2010) argues that while the protestant work ethic was central to the mass-production economy, there is a new kind of work ethic behind the knowledge-economy—the hacker ethic. The term hacker not only refers to computer scientists but also to anyone following few guiding principles. The first guiding value in a hacker's life is passion, that is, some intrinsically interesting and fulfilling pursuit. The second value is that the hacker work ethic consists of melding passion with freedom. Hackers have flexible work patterns and are not constrained by the traditional 9 to 5. They have no work hours restraints as long as they do their 70 to 90 hours a week. Bill Gates frequently brags about his experience of coding for 72-hours straight without sleeping. The third value is that peer recognition is equally, if not more, important than money. "We never did it for the money" said every billionaire in the Silicon Valley. For hackers, the frontier between work and leisure is blurred to the extent that the traditional work week doesn't apply to them. Like many of my fellow millennials, I regard weekends as opportunities for self-improvement and having the time to write this book. My brother, who studies industrial design, spends his weekends working on designing cool products and publishing new projects on Kickstarter and his website. Hackers have a mission. The hacker ethic is an extension of the Protestant ethic in that work is central to self-actualization; however, unlike the Sisyphusian Protestant ethic, work has to be fun, meaningful, and for oneself.

In conclusion, there is a strong and growing trend toward living, working, dating, and playing in urban areas. The decline of suburban appeal will intensify until the next technological revolution occurs. Indeed, one can imagine the massive adoption of new technologies such as self-driving cars, holograms, and robotization that will make distance less relevant than it is today. Although some scholars predicted the end of cities with the advent of ICTs, cities will only lose their value with an advance in transportation technologies. Indeed, the tramways, the metro lines, and the automobiles were the backbone of   suburbanization.

3

FROM INDUSTRIAL PARKS TO INNOVATION DISTRICTS

In 1890, British economist Alfred Marshall published an influential book titled *The Principles of Economics* in which he modeled the concept of the industrial district and localization economy. Marshall describes how an agglomeration, or cluster, of small- and medium- sized firms, such as those in Lancashire and Sheffield, fosters the development of external economies (Belussi & Sedita, 2010). Marshall (1920) observed that "the mysteries of the trade become no mysteries; but are as it were in the air, and children learn many of them unconsciously." He laid the foundations to further investigate externalities, returns to scale, economics of agglomeration, and spillovers. More than 100 years after the first publication of Marshall's book, the study of industrial districts and their effects has increased in popularity. Marshall's external economies can be found in various disciplines, such as industrial economics, business studies, economic geography, sociology, urban planning, social network analysis, and political science (Belussi & Sedita, 2010). Marshall's observations led to the conceptualization of economics zones, namely industrial parks, special economic zones, eco-industrial parks, technology parks, and the more recent innovation districts.

The appropriate growth strategy for any country, region, or city depends on where it is located relative to its stage of competitive development. Technological catch-up by building industrial parks and Special Economic Zones are easy solutions for low-income countries to deliver rapid economic growth. Once a country has achieved middle-income status, however, the competitive priority has to be on innovation and sustainability in order to efficiently compete in the knowledge economy. Technological catch-up is much easier than building the infrastructure and creating the policies to compete in the knowledge-economy. Industrial parks are the simplest form of planned estates and will appeal to countries that are at a low stage of economic development. Special Economic Zones are more difficult to put in place and require the appropriate infrastructure, such as airports and ports, and an efficient legal regulatory framework for customs and duties. SEZs are successful when countries are not well integrated in the global trade. As countries develop, however, they become more and more integrated with trade blocks and multi-national organizations, which has the effect of limiting the benefits that stem from SEZs. Eco-Industrial Zones are the next economic zone for countries to implement when they reach higher stages of economic development. As countries achieve a higher stage of economic development, there are also stronger environmental regulations, which make eco-industrial zones not only necessary to comply with environmental regulations, but also financially profitable for the industries. Technology parks are the economic zones adopted by urban and regional leaders who wish to compete in the knowledge economy. Innovation districts are the most sophisticated economic zones in which the production of new knowledge and the concept of sustainability are central elements in their success. The most advanced countries have eco-industrial parks, technology parks, and innovation districts (e.g. Singapore, Switzerland, the United States, and so on), while low-income countries have only industrial parks or SEZs (e.g. Cambodia, Ethiopia, Kenya, and so on).

The first industrial parks were established in Western Europe and the United States in the late nineteenth- and early twentieth-century. Trafford industrial park, which opened in 1896 near Manchester in the United Kingdom, is the first planned industrial park in the world (World Bank, 1992). Planned industrial parks like Trafford industrial park, for instance, were aiming to replicate the spontaneous growth through market forces of the industrial districts described by Alfred Marshall (1920). The establishment of industrial parks as an economic development strategy was popular in Western Europe, the USSR, and the United States in the 1950s until the end of the 1970s. The first generation of industrial parks was driven by public sector development and was operated with government subsidies. The industrial parks were fairly simple—offering only basic infrastructure and facilities—compared to the diversity and sophistication of recent industrial parks. Indeed, over the decades, the scope of services and facilities provided by industrial parks became more sophisticated and holistic. In the 1970s, structural changes—namely the oil crisis, information and communication technology, and globalization—led industries in developed countries to outsource their production to developing and emerging countries. Industrial parks became a successful development strategy for developing and emerging countries to attract FDI and foreign industries. The model is particularly popular in China, as well as Southeast Asian countries, where labor is cheap and abundant. In the most advanced economies, industrial parks, which were once necessary for competitiveness in the mass-production economy, now have been replaced by technology parks in the knowledge economy.

The technology parks phenomena was initiated in 1951 when Dean Frederick Terman established the Stanford Research Park near Stanford University, which later became the center of the Silicon Valley. The idea originates in the linear model of innovation, which led to the creation of scientific communities to generate innovation. In 1959, Research Triangle Park in North Carolina was established as a strategy to foster economic growth in a depressed region (Phillimore & Joseph, 2003). Until the 1970s, technology parks were a North American phenomenon, designed to serve the needs of entrepreneurially minded academics and the promotion of new technology, while at the same time leveraging the power of university-industry linkages (Anttiroiko, 2004). The idea spread across the United States after Stanford Research Park became the standard for science-based industrial development. The Japanese took the concept of technology parks a bit further by developing science-cities in the 1970s, with, for instance, Tsukuba Science City. The first technology parks were created in Europe in the early 1970s with Sophia-Antipolis in France and Cambridge in England (Anttiroiko, 2004; Quintas, Wield, & Massey, 1992). Since the 1980s, technology parks have been a trendy economic development strategy for fostering new industrial dynamics in developed and emerging countries. However, building innovative or creative clusters is a long and slow process, and all have uncertain fates (Hall, 2004). The Research Triangle Park, for instance, was around for three decades before it was considered a success. Indeed, the technology park was still regarded as a failed experiment as late as 1987 (Miller & Coté, 1987).

Technology parks, also known as research parks and science parks, are economic zones aiming to foster new industrial growth—in terms of jobs and production—by attracting high technology manufacturing firms into a privileged estate (Castells & Hall, 1994). The basic function of the technology parks is to generate the tools for cities to compete in the informational or knowledge economy (Castells & Hall, 1994). The underlying assumption is that regions and cities can prosper only if they have some level of linkage to the production of innovation (Castells & Hall, 1994). The technology parks are created when there is the right environment and support from the local, regional, or national authorities. The right environment entails the presence of "research and training institutions, favorable tax and credit incentives, availability of industrial land, a local labor market with quality engineers and technicians, a good transportation system, and adequate telecommunications" (Castells & Hall, 1994, p.110). Environmental quality, bureaucratic flexibility, and a good locational image also enhance the attractiveness of technology parks (Castells & Hall, 1994). In addition, the role of governments and universities seems to be crucial for the establishment and growth of technology parks. Regions and cities are more flexible than countries when adapting to changing conditions of markets, technology, and culture. Indeed, cities have a greater response capacity to generate "targeted development projects, negotiate with multinational firms, foster the growth of small and medium endogenous firms, and create conditions that will attract new sources of wealth, power, and prestige" (Castells & Hall, 1994).

The Silicon Valley is often viewed as a template for technology parks' initiatives for policy-makers and urban leaders around the world. Urban leaders and politicians from across the globe frequently organize study tours in the Silicon Valley to learn and to replicate the model. It is often said that the only high-technology cluster in the world not trying to imitate the Silicon Valley is the Silicon Valley. Skolkovo near Moscow and Paris-Saclay near Paris are two megaprojects that have replicating the Silicon Valley as their mission statements. Peter Hall (1998) demonstrates that two cities in the world—namely Tokyo and the Silicon Valley—have succeeded over the past 50 years or so at generating highly successful and innovative ecosystems. These two cities, however, have emerged from two distinct development patterns. Tokyo has emerged with heavy state involvement, while the Silicon Valley has emerged from the entrepreneurs' desire to build the next multi-billion dollar companies. Although these two innovative milieux are both highly successful, the Silicon Valley is seen as easier to replicate than Tokyo. The apparent structural complexity and heavy state involvement make Tokyo a difficult and expensive innovative milieu to replicate. The Silicon Valley's model was so ingrained in planners' imaginations that suburban technology parks were seen as the only possible strategy to produce a successful innovation ecosystem. The first knowledge intensive companies to rediscover the cities—of Berlin, Boston, New York, San Francisco, London, Paris, and so on—as convenient locations were the internet startups of the late 1990s. Startups were looking for cheap spaces in a convenient location with plenty of urban amenities for informal and formal meetings. The suburban technology parks were unaffordable for many startups and didn't provide the fun and excitement of the city. Moreover, suburban technology parks are established locations, and therefore locating your startup in one of them automatically makes you part of the establishment. In an effort to be edgy, startups became pioneers and the inner city became their rediscovered frontier. Innovation districts and creative districts are initiatives that aim to mimic spontaneous innovation ecosystems that have emerged through market forces in the late 1990s during the rise of the knowledge economy. Those initiatives work as artificial reefs nurturing emerging innovation ecosystems. While suburban technology parks were, until recently, the preferred method for knowledge location, inner-city initiatives are becoming increasingly popular. Knowledge hubs are being developed as part of the urban fabric—rather than isolated Greenfield projects that are outside towns—and they tend to become mixed in terms of function. The creative hubs are not mono-functional business parks, and can be found in city centers or regenerated industrial areas (van Winden et al., 2013). Work and life are mixed up in time and space and have an urban locus that fits the needs of the people working there. These urban technology parks are multifaceted, where the boundaries between physical, digital, economic, social, and cultural spaces are blurred, and are simultaneously focused on regional resilience, entrepreneurship, and innovation (Clark et al., 2010). They are the result of strategies that aim to develop creative places within the urban center, whether they are in historical centers, in old industrial and logistical areas, or downtown. The main idea behind this concept is that cities can use science, technology, design, arts, culture, media, and engineering as driving forces of urban regeneration and economic development (Da Cunha & Selada, 2009). Knowledge occurs at the level of the inner city in an interactive and unplanned process in which the different stakeholders combine knowledge and competencies (van Winden et al., 2013). Moreover, the trend toward open innovation and collaboration is more fruitful in the city than in bland suburban technology parks. The planning of specific locations where the knowledge economy can unfold has become one of the most visible initiatives of local governments worldwide. These urban areas that are at the center of urban strategies and policies are part of the trend called "the knowledge turn in urban policy" (van Winden et al., 2013).

The paradigm-shift from mass-production to knowledge-production in the developed economies implies that there is a reorganization of the productive apparatus for the promotion of knowledge-intensive activities. The growing focus on knowledge, innovation, and creativity—along with the trends toward globalization, sustainability, open innovation, communications, and media technologies—make inner cities attractive again. Cities have capitalized on this trend to build technology parks with an urban focus that specializes in knowledge, innovation, creativity, and continuous learning. The concepts of knowledge cities (Carrillo, 2004), intelligent cities (Komninos, 2002), innovative cities (Simmie, 2013), creative cities (Florida, 2002; Landry, 2000), ihubs (Da Cunha & Selada, 2009), innovation districts (Barcelona, 2000), multimedia cities (Duarte & Sabaté, 2013), and media cities (Mould, 2014) have been adopted to some extent as strategic urban policies in diverse cities around the world. In the recent past, urban policies have shifted away from a strict focus on knowledge intensive industries and now incorporate the creative industries, which emerged as a promising growth sector with a strong urban orientation. Urban technology districts, moreover, are increasingly seen as powerful catalysts for urban regeneration. Cities implementing these initiatives envision a future based on knowledge as a means to achieve a successful urban transition into the 21st century.

Manuel Castells (1989) argued that a technological revolution of "historic proportions is transforming the fundamental dimensions of human life: time and space." Some people have speculated that the advent of globalization and the rise of ICT will cause the world to become flat; that place will not matter and geography will be dead (Cairncross, 1997). Cities are discovering that location does matter, and it matters more today than ever before (Begg, 2002; Feld, 2012; Florida, 2002). The death of geography thesis has over estimated the distance-destroying capacity of ICT by conflating spatial reach with social depth (Morgan, 2004). Over the last 30 years, the growth experience of American cities has varied widely. The population of some cities has grown significantly, while other cities virtually disappeared (Glaeser, Scheinkman, & Shleifer, 1995). We are experiencing a competition between cities, regions, and nations—as well as firms—with clear winners and losers (Clark et al., 2004). The revolutionary nature of ICT has reinforced the economic power of a number of key cities due to the highly localized nature of knowledge-intensive activities.

At the heart of urban competitiveness strategies are urban regeneration policies, which became popular in the European Union at the turn of the 21st century. These programs could be labeled as gentrification (Smith, 2002). Gentrification is a process that involves "the transition of inner-city neighborhoods from a status of relative poverty and limited property investment to a state of commodification and reinvestment" (Ley, 2003). The refurbished neighborhood population structure changes from working-class to upper-middle-class. In Manhattan, SoHo and the Lower East Side are examples of such radical gentrification. Gentrification was first localized in rich world cities such as New York City, London, Paris, and Sydney and is today a widespread phenomenon that exists even in emerging countries' cities such as Mumbai and São Paulo (Smith, 2002). In the 1980s, states started to cut subsidies and gentrification began to rest on real estate development companies and public-private partnerships (Harvey, 2012). The restructuring of the city along private interests embodies the wider global transformations taking place (Smith, 1996). Competition between cities implies standards by which to compare them. These standards include the availability of urban amenities, as well as the quality of professional, cultural, and social life. Gentrification around the world—whether in Le Marais in Paris or in the Lower East Side in Manhattan—looks remarkably similar, with common characteristics including third wave coffee shops, burger bars, hip restaurants, lofts, and international clientele and residents. Innovation districts' managers have to be careful not to polarize the city between innovative haves and have-nots. Innovation districts must be designed with the goal of being as inclusive as possible in order to avoid the risk of a public backlash that could put the development of the district in jeopardy.

Brynjolfsson, McAfee, and Spence (2014) argue that in our knowledge economy the scarcest and hence most valuable resource will be neither ordinary labor nor ordinary capital, but rather people who can "create new ideas and innovations." The authors point out that "digital technologies increasingly make both ordinary labor and ordinary capital commodities, and so a greater share of the rewards from ideas will go to the creators, innovators, and entrepreneurs. People with ideas, not workers or investors, will be the scarcest resource." It is because innovation districts cater to people with ideas and help them generate new ideas that they are so important in the knowledge economy.

In conclusion, innovation districts are the byproducts of three converging factors: the paradigm-shift from mass-production to the knowledge economy, the rise of spontaneous innovation ecosystems in inner-city areas such as Cambridge (Massachusetts), the Silicon Alley (New York), and the Silicon Sentier (Paris), and the social changes that are making living downtown a transformative experience once again. The concept of an innovation district emerged from the imitation of successful urban milieux. Today's innovation districts work as artificial reefs nurturing emerging innovation ecosystems, and aim to replicate the spontaneous growth that was achieved through market forces in the original innovation districts.

4

WHAT ARE INNOVATION DISTRICTS?

The previous chapters describe the re-emergence of city centers and the emergence of innovation districts as urban economic development strategies to capitalize on the knowledge-based information economy. This chapter will define what exactly innovation districts are. First, innovation districts foster innovation at the city level and for that matter are resilient urban milieux. Innovation districts share similar goals. The cities' objectives when implementing innovation districts are: (1) to develop or redevelop an unproductive part of the city; (2) to attract, create, or retain talented individuals and innovative companies; and (3) to become or remain an innovation hub. Innovation districts can be defined as top-down urban innovation ecosystems that combine urban planning, productive, collaborative, and creative environments, all coordinated under a strong leadership, with the ultimate objectives of accelerating the innovation process and of strengthening the location's competitiveness. Innovation districts are urban development strategies that are endorsed by municipal leaderships. An Innovation district is not a spontaneous occurrence in that the city always plays a large part in its creation.

Innovation districts, however, are spontaneous innovation ecosystems in that they have emerged through market forces without any formal planning from the city. The Silicon Alley in New York City and the Silicon Sentier in Paris are such examples of spontaneous innovation districts. Innovation districts are self-sustaining and versatile innovation ecosystems. In the innovation district's framework, municipal leadership will pilot the development of the district for 10 to 15 years in order to transform the artificial innovation district into a self-sustaining innovation district. Innovation districts work as artificial reefs nurturing emerging innovative ecosystems.

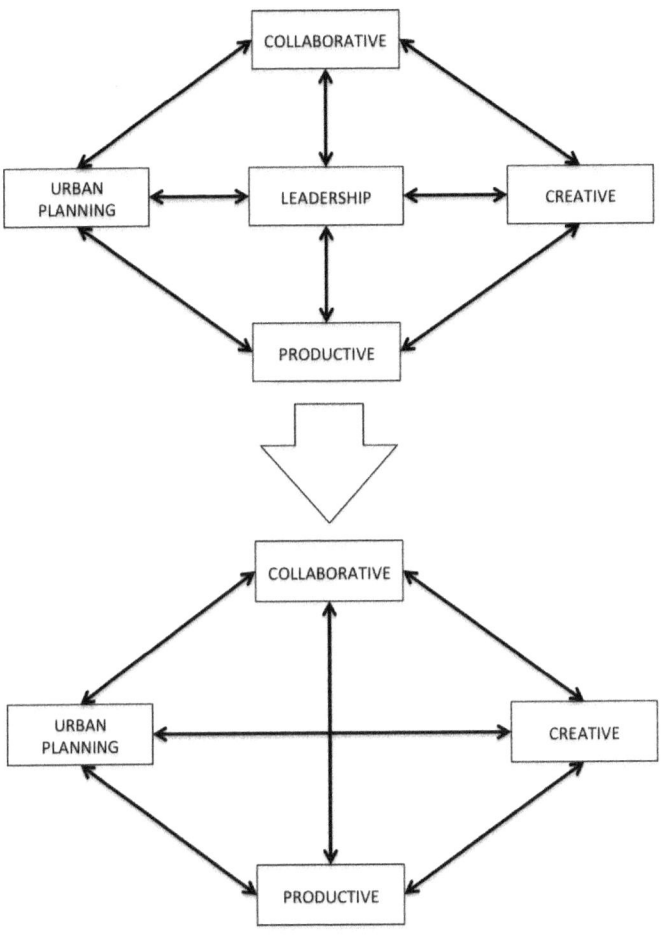

Figure 1. From artificial innovation districts to self-sustaining innovation districts.

In the innovation district's framework, each of the layers of innovation interact with one another, creating a feedback loop that reinforces a location's innovative capacity. These feedback loops reinforce the innovative capacities of both the firms and the individuals living in the innovation district. Local governments developing innovation districts can in turn affect the sophistication of the framework, and thus their cities' innovative capacities, by upgrading the different processes in any of the five layers of innovation.

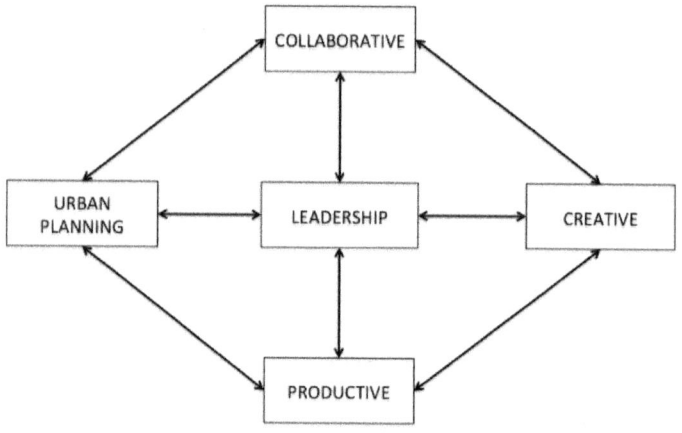

Figure 2. The innovation district's framework.

The five layers of innovation have to be developed in the following order: (1) leadership, (2) urban planning, (3) productive, (4) collaborative, and (5) creative.

(1)   Leadership

Leadership refers to the municipal organization that is going to facilitate the district's transformation into a self-sustaining innovation district. This municipal body needs to have sufficient financial and human resources to be able to pilot the following functions: managing landing platforms, managing spaces for collaboration, connecting entrepreneurs with venture capitalists, providing coaching and mentoring, designing the district's masterplan, providing funds for startups, organizing cultural events, workshops, training, advertising, marketing, etc. The municipal organizations should be free from the local political instability and have a sustainable source of funding for a period of 10 to 15 years. The city's political parties must be united and be committed to the innovation district's success. The leadership structure has to coordinate the different layers of innovation in order to generate a self-sustaining innovation ecosystem.

(2) Urban Planning

Urban planning is the second layer of innovation. It refers to the urban characteristics that are deemed attractive to innovators and that facilitate the process of innovation. Urban planners are innovation masterplanners. Urban planners should focus their talent on designing a district that is dense, compact, walkable, bikable, and mixed-use, while at the same time favorable to a high quality of life with parks, a thriving street-culture, and vibrant nightlife.

(3) Productive

In the productive framework, the question to ask is what types of industries do we want in the district. The first critical element is that the district must be for knowledge-intensive companies. The second critical element is that the district is a place for entrepreneurs and startups. Both of these elements must be present in order for the district to be considered an innovation district. The question urban leaders have to ask themselves is whether they want a cluster-based development approach or a diversity-based development approach.

(4)   Collaborative

The collaborative layer refers to the capacity of the district to foster collaboration between individuals and firms, and between universities, institutions, and private companies; it also refers to the ability of the district to accelerate the turnover of ideas, as well as spinoffs of existing companies and the creation of new startups. The collaborative layer relies on the presence of universities, public institutions, supporting institutions, and spaces for collaboration (SFC).

(5)   Creative

The creative layer is what liberates individuals to experiment and try new ways of doing things. It is the byproduct of two theories, that of the creative milieu and that of the creative class. The district must have cultural facilities such as a library, a museum, a concert venue, graffiti walls, and artists' workshops; third places such as bars, restaurants, indie coffee shops, and exclusive shops also must be present; finally, there need to be pop-up events such as street musicians, street artists, ephemeral sculptures, ephemeral bars and restaurants. The creative milieu will attract the creative class, which in turn will enhance the quality of the creative milieu.

It is highly unlikely that a city can improve the innovative capacity of one of its districts by relying on only one layer of innovation. It is when the five layers of innovation are employed simultaneously that a district's innovative capacity is strengthened. In addition, it must be stressed that the five layers of innovation interact with one another and are insidiously interlinked. In the next chapter, I will detail each process of the five layers of innovation.

5

THE INNOVATION PROCESSES

The innovation district's framework is a product of many different models that were theorized as beneficial to innovation. Although frameworks simplify the complexity of reality, they are powerful tools that are easily adopted by policymakers. In this chapter, I will outline the different processes of the framework that make the innovation district, an innovation district. Some processes taken independently don't improve a city's innovative capacity but it is when they interact with other processes that they form an innovative whole. Innovation districts produce an innovative outcome that is greater than the sum of the innovative processes. The five layers of innovation are: (1) leadership, (2) urban planning, (3) productive, (4) collaborative, and (5) creative. There are several processes involves for each of the five layers of innovation. The innovation district is the product of hundreds of processes.

LEADERSHIP

(1) Leadership includes the city (mayor's office and municipal departments), real estate development companies, private companies, universities, the civil society, maverick entrepreneurs, and branding.

The impulse to create an innovation district can come from the city (local government, mayor's office), universities, real-estate development companies, private companies, the civil society, or maverick entrepreneurs. However, no matter what, municipal governments always have to back the initiative. No innovation district can be successful without a strong municipal support. When the initiative comes from the city, the project has to be supported by the civil society, private companies, real-estate companies, universities, and entrepreneurs. The early stage discussion has to involve those different actors and all need to participate in the debate.

The city, namely the mayor's office and municipal departments, is the primary instigator in deciding to create an innovation district. In Barcelona, Boston, Medellin, and Singapore, with 22@ Barcelona, Boston's Innovation District, Ruta N Medellin, and one-north Singapore, leadership originated within the local government bodies. The mayors of Barcelona and Boston, Joan Clos and Thomas Menino, were driven by a strong vision to build an unconventional district rather than building the conventional condominiums, shopping malls, and office towers prized by real-estate companies.

Real estate companies are driven by profits. They don't usually initiate in unconventional thinking except when the benefits exceed the costs. The benefits to participate in the innovation district's trend for real-estate companies tend to exceed the costs. Knowledge workers have a high purchasing power and want to live downtown. In Boston, it took

Thomas Menino, few arguments to convince real-estate companies to incorporate innovative elements into their master plans when planning for the innovation district.

Two **maverick entrepreneurs** have recently transformed part of their cities into wannabe innovation districts. Tony Hsieh, CEO of Zappos, has founded the Downtown Project in Las Vegas. Dan Gilbert, founder of Quicken loans, has contributed to the revitalization of downtown Detroit. Those two initiatives have in common that both Tony Hsieh and Dan Gilbert have built their innovation districts to attract and retain the best employees for Zappos and Quickens loans. Entrepreneurial efforts to impulse innovation are not limited to the United States. In Paris, France, Xavier Niel has launched in 2013 a tech school that covers tuition for 1,000 students every year. In 2016, Niel will inaugurate the largest startups incubator in the world. The incubator will be located in the Halle Freyssinet, an old train station reconverted into a hip space for collaboration. While remarkable, those entrepreneurial endeavors are not supported enough by local governments to their full potential.

Civil society and private companies have to be consulted when planning innovation districts. As any unconventional initiatives, some people will be reticent to back the project to create an innovation district, other will argue to stop the project justifying their claims by saying that the innovation district will increase inequalities, favor gentrification, and will fail to deliver anything except increasing the local taxes. Those NIMBYism—Not In My Back Yard—claims are legitimate and should be answered with concrete responses. The civil society and private companies have to participate in the discussion on how to resolve such potential setbacks by having a say on which building to preserve, on the percentage of social housing to be allocated, on the potential costs and benefits coming from the future innovation district.

Universities play a pivotal role in the success of innovation districts and as such, should have an active role in the planning of the district. The role of universities is amplified in the productive and collaborative layers. Indeed, universities provide the fuel for innovations with future entrepreneurs, talented graduates, entrepreneurial professors, and seed capital for startups. Universities will have a more or less important role depending on the strategy adopted by the city for its innovation district.

When the innovation district is finally launched, the organization in charge of piloting the district has to provide continuous support and has to brand and advertise the district to outsiders and innovative companies around the world. Branding has to revolve around three axes: branding for the creative class/entrepreneurs, branding for innovative companies, and branding for real-estate development companies. The branding for creative class and entrepreneurs has to focus on quality of life, the easiness to create new ventures, and the spaces for collaboration that are present in the innovation district. A good communication strategy would be to interview successful entrepreneurs from other cities and countries that have established themselves in the innovation district. Entrepreneurs and the creative class are more mobile than ever before. They thrive on new experiences and long to live in vibrant cities where the action is. The branding to attract innovative companies should aim to demonstrate the easiness of doing business in the innovation district as well as the easiness to recruit talented and hardworking workers. The branding for real estate should appeal to their core functions to experiment with new architectural approaches and build flagship projects that will give them worldwide recognition. A real-estate package with the relevant information, real-estate trends, municipal support, and possible tax-exemptions should be made available. The innovation district website should provide the needed and relevant information for entrepreneurs, graduates, creative class, young professionals, innovative companies, and the real estate development companies.

URBAN PLANNING

(2) For an innovation district, urban planners have to devote their energy to designing a district that is propitious to innovative thinking. This can be achieved by making the district more efficient with SMART infrastructures; more open and accessible with public transportation; more authentic with rehabilitating old factories and warehouses; more diverse with mixed-use planning; more dense and compact through new zoning laws; more vibrant with restaurants, bars, and nightlife; more green with a system of parks, pedestrian-friendly corridors, and bike lanes; and more symbolic with iconic buildings. The objectives of urban planning in an innovation district are twofold: to promote a great quality of life

that will attract the creative class and knowledge workers and to encourage serendipitous encounters that will enable them to collaborate and exchange ideas. The combination of these two objectives will foster an atmosphere beneficial to risky and innovative thinking.

Innovation districts are mixed-use districts. The functionalist movement to plan whole cities with single-use zoning, with Brasilia as its most famous example, has served its purpose. The use of single zoning in urban planning was adopted on a massive scale after World War II and is still the predominant tool of urban planning. Single-use zoning proponents offer a vision of a city that, based on its master plan, appears attractive. From above, the city seems to be as efficiently built as an assembly line where each area has its purpose and each purpose has its area. It is no coincidence that mass production and single zoning became ubiquitous at the same time. As well as its similarity to an assembly line in which economic and social life are streamlined, single zoning is also a powerful tool for social control.

In the Western world and in the USSR after WWII, while the Western elites feared the spread of communism, the Politburo feared overthrow. For both types of regimes, single zoning lessened social ties and fostered individualism, both of which diminished social unrest. As expected, the countries today (think China) that are massively adopting single zoning are authoritarian regimes. As noted, single zoning has served its purpose as an efficient assembly line for the mass-production economy, but we are living in a knowledge economy, and communism is, thankfully, an ideology of the past. Mixed-use districts, where young and old, poor and rich, students and professionals, entrepreneurs and office workers, designers and researchers live and work in the same area have to be the planners' priority. The intensity of interactions and diversity, however, can be achieved only in a confined space within a city——the city's innovation district.

Indeed, diversity and interactions should not be imposed on a city's residents as a norm but as an opportunity. People like what is familiar to them and, consequently, like living in a neighborhood in which other residents are similar to them. Innovation districts, however, appeal to risk-takers and diversity seekers who represent a minority of the population. Ideally, the population breakdown of an innovation district should be as follows: creative and knowledge workers, 30%; entrepreneurs, 10%; artists, 5%; students, 15%; employees (office, municipal, and service workers), 30%; retirees and unemployed, 10%. The ratio of entrepreneurs, creative, and knowledge workers compared to the rest of the people living in the district should be 1:1. This 1:1 ratio serves a number of functions. It increases the visibility of entrepreneurs, artists, and knowledge workers in order to inspire the rest of the district's population to create, to take risks, and to innovate. It reminds the entrepreneurs, artists, and knowledge workers that they form a whole with society and that they should not live in an innovative/creative ivory tower. Additionally, it builds sufficient critical mass to cross-fertilize ideas and facilitate the exchange of information among entrepreneurs, artists, knowledge workers, and the rest of the district's population. In opposition to technology and business parks, mixed-use innovation districts are open and lively districts twenty-four hours a day, seven days a week, and innovation districts feature a constant flow of people that contributes to both a vibrant social and cultural scene and a sense of safety.

Innovation districts must be designed as open systems. Innovation districts must be fully open to outsiders. In opposition to gated communities and technology parks that are built as closed systems, innovation districts should be easily accessible to anyone. An innovation district should be located next to the urban downtown (10 to 15 minutes radius from downtown by public transportation), reliant on multimodal transportation systems (public transportation, private cars, bike lanes, walking) and, ideally, connected to the rest of the city through metro lines, public buses, and trams. A connected node of transportation should be within a maximum of ten minutes' walk from any location within the district. Public bike-share services and electric cars (such as Velib and Autolib in Paris) should be made available within the innovation district. The ratio of private cars to public transportation for accessing the innovation district should be 1:4; that is, for one person driving a private car, four people should be using public transportation, biking, or walking. The use of public transportation should be encouraged because it favors exchange of information and knowledge formally through participating in private discussions or informally through listening to private conversations. An innovation district is an open system and, as such, is easily accessible to everyone.

Innovation districts are efficient. Tools such as SMART infrastructures and the use of Geographic Information Systems (GIS) can make innovation districts more efficient. The design of the innovation district, however, shouldn't revolve around the ICT as in Songdo in South Korea. For its real estate developers, the South Korean city of Songdo is the largest and state-of-the-art "smart city"; however, its design is flawed. The entire city, master planned from scratch, was intended to house around 300,000 inhabitants, but a discrepancy exists between the rate of obsolescence of its buildings and that of its networks. The integrated network in Songdo currently promoted by its developers is innovative today, but it won't be in ten years. Cities must be resilient to new technologies, but they cannot be built entirely around new technologies.

Cities must, however, invest in infrastructures that have a high return on investment (fifteen to twenty years). Improvements such as a pneumatic waste collection system and sensors to reduce energy and water consumption should be prioritized after rigorous cost-benefit calculations for the city and its inhabitants. Smart infrastructures do not make cities more innovative, but they do allow for more efficiency, thus accelerating the process of innovation when the right processes of the framework are present.

Innovation districts feel authentic. Urban

planning must pay special attention to preserving existing heritage sites and historical buildings with a goal of creating an atmosphere that feels unique and nurtures a district's distinct identity. Warehouses and factories can be retrofitted as coworking spaces for entrepreneurs, spaces for collaboration, restaurants, coffee shops, microbreweries, workshops, lofts, or micro-apartments. Innovation districts are the cities' new icons. The innovation district creates a new centrality in the city as 22@ Barcelona did with the Torre Agbar, designed by architect Jean Nouvel, or Boston's Innovation District with the Institute for Contemporary Arts (ICA). Iconic buildings create a new centrality.

The built environment insidiously influences people. The vast majority of technology parks and business districts are bland spaces with their cookie-cutter buildings and sets of amenities. Such bland, closed systems can hinder employees' creativity and productivity. For example, for most employees working in technology or business parks a major challenge is to leave as early as possible to beat the traffic. Traffic jams and transportation are prime topics of conversation among employees whose lack of motivation undermines companies' profitability. (The movie *Office Space* satirizes the work lives of employees in suburban business parks.) Technology and business parks made sense in a mass-production age in which the roles played by individuals in the production processes were restricted. However, in the knowledge economy, knowledge workers are central, and to make them flourish, they need a stimulating environment that rewards risk and experimentation.

Innovation districts reward bold architecture and innovative design, encouraging people to be more bold and innovative. One's identity changes along with that of the district. The way people perceive individuals changes, which changes how individuals see themselves. When someone says to an individual, "I live in city Y's Innovation District," that person will see that individual as more innovative, which will encourage that individual to become more innovative. In psychology, living in an innovation district is a self-fulfilling prophecy. Conservative districts breed conservative thinking. Innovative districts breed innovative thinking.

Innovation districts are dense and compact. The concepts of compact cities and eco-cities were developed to tackle rising concerns about climate change expressed by international organizations, the general public, and national and local governments. The intention of compact cities is to become sustainable as defined in the "Brundtland Report" (WCED, 1987) and the Rio Earth Summit (UNCED, 1992). Cities are one cause of environmental degradation, a rising ecological footprint, and resource depletion (Jenks & Burgess, 2000). Urban sprawl is seen as the root of environmental degradation and is used as an antonym for compactness (Gordon & Richardson, 1997). Urban sprawl, for instance, induces around 60% more commuting time than does urban compactness (Gordon & Richardson, 1997). The way cities are planned has a tremendous impact on sustainability. Burton, Jenks, and Williams (2013) highlight the positive role of urban features on sustainability including size, shape, density, compactness, land use, zoning policies, layout and building features, green areas, and open spaces. The compact city takes on different meanings, each with different planning implications. Compactness can be applied at the level of the metropolitan area, the inner city, the specific district, or the central business district (CBD) [Gordon & Richardson, 1997]. Density, intensification, and compactness imply that public transportation will be enhanced and that commute distance and CO_2 emissions will be reduced. A sustainable city has a form and scale that is appropriate for walking, cycling, and efficient public transport and encourages social interactions (Burton, Jenks, & Williams, 2003). Compact cities enable more efficient use of amenities and systems such as public and private transportation, waste management that, in turn, improves urban living standards and quality of life (Jenks & Burgess, 2000).

In developing countries, denser living environments are associated with negative externalities such as pollution, traffic congestion, noise, proximity to hazardous waste sites, diseases from contaminated water, and overloaded sanitation systems (Jenks & Burgess, 2000). Inadequate infrastructures and lenient environmental laws and controls amplify those negative externalities. However, higher densities also reflect traditional patterns of social organization more favorable to community life and interpersonal cooperation; thus, living in dense cities inside developing countries is more social, genuine, and convivial, despite lower standards of living. It is more socially rewarding to live in a "dense developing country city than (to live) in the affluent suburbs of the United States" (Jenks & Burgess, 2000).

High density, the main attribute of a compact city, positively affects social interaction, learning, and innovation. Jane Jacobs (1961) was one of the first urban theorists to revive advocacy for high urban density at a time when low density was seen as a way to improve quality of life. High density was a pervasive feature of cities until the automobile and rapid transportation were made widely available. Dense neighborhoods had serious functional weaknesses in the mid-twentieth century since they had been designed when the automobile did not exist and, consequently, "were unpleasant places to drive and impossible places to park" (Storper, 2013). At the same time, growing sprawl made the automobile indispensable (Storper, 2013).

For Jacobs (1961), dense neighborhoods led to serendipitous contacts among city residents. Urban neighborhoods thrive when they have between one and two hundred households per acre (Jacobs, 1961). For Jacobs (1961), cities should at least have a hundred homes per acre to generate enough street traffic to support social interactions and exciting urban amenities such as nightlife. Dense cities have to coincide with the right urban systems and structures to positively affect quality of life. City travel, for instance, depends on the kind of urban systems in place. If you "create more road spaces, you get more cars; if you create more bike lanes, you get more bikes; if you make more space for people, you get more people and of course then you get public life"

(Montgomery, 2013).

Edward Glaeser (2011) argues that dense cities foster the necessary interactions for economic innovation and technological progress. Land use restrictions should be eased to foster innovation. Rates of patents and innovation are higher in dense metropolitan areas than elsewhere (Storper, 2013). Alfred Marshall (1920) has conceptualized the positive role of externalities in industrial districts. These externalities are stronger in dense districts because density facilitates the flow of ideas. Patent intensity and the per-capita invention rate are positively related to the density of employment in the denser districts of metropolitan areas (Carlino, 2001). For instance, during the 1990s the number of patents was significantly greater in metropolitan statistical areas (MSA) with denser local economies. The number of patents per capita is, on average, 20% to 30% higher in an MSA whose local economy is twice as dense as that of another MSA (Carlino, 2001). Patent intensity is maximized at an employment density of about 2,200 jobs per square mile (Carlino, Chatterjee, & Hunt, 2007). The densest cities are faster at spreading ideas that, in turn, produce innovation and economic growth (Carlino et al., 2007).

The quality of density is also essential for generating positive externalities. The density of creative workers is also a determining factor in spurring regional innovation (Knudsen, Florida, Gates, & Stolarick, 2007). Regression analysis finds a positive relationship between the density of creative workers and metropolitan patenting activity (Knudsen et al., 2007), suggesting that density is a significant factor in nurturing knowledge spillovers and innovations. Dense cities facilitate learning among individuals, and the diversity of human interactions in dense cities generates faster learning and daily experimentation. While cities generate a high innovation rate, their primary objective is to create learning opportunities for residents (Glaeser 1999). Dense urban agglomerations foster interactions and serendipitous encounters among residents that facilitate learning (Glaeser 1999). Residents of dense neighborhoods acquire more skills from each other than residents from diffuse neighborhoods. The premium paid to live in dense cities, such as a higher rent and a lower quality of life, is compensated for by the new skills that individuals acquire by interacting with other residents (Glaeser 1999). As a result, dense cities offer a unique environment to increase the speed of interactions for informal learning from social and business contacts and to facilitate networking (Glaeser 1999). Cities attract risk-takers who benefit most from learning new skills and, as a consequence, "urbanization increases when the demand for skills increases" (Glaeser 1999).

Innovation districts are vibrant. They are filled with hip restaurants, third-wave coffee shops, funky bars on rooftops, and nightspots. The vibrancy of the innovation district fulfills two purposes: to facilitate exchange of knowledge and to attract the young, creative class. The restaurants, bars, coffee shops, and so on are "third places" where the creative class can work or organize informal meetings. The boundary between work and personal life has disappeared; thus, third places are spaces to exchange information, to network, and to find potential clients or partners. While writing this book I visited my local coffee shop, and a group of three girls sat next to me (lucky me). Serendipitously for me, they were meeting for the first time to discuss a partnership between a sushi restaurant chain and a famous sushi blog. This informal meeting in a coffee shop, in which I indirectly took part, exemplifies how third places encourage the spread of knowledge. Additionally, informal meetings in third places reinforce trust among participants because they meet on neutral ground; the informal meeting does not feel like a business negotiation but a collaboration in which everyone wins.

Innovation districts are green and walkable. The innovation district's master plan should be similar to Patrick Geddes' master plan for Tel Aviv—organic with an integrated system of small parks and meeting points. The street blocks have to be frequent and differ in size and space to include more diversity in the master plan. Walkability is a priority for an innovation district master plan. To be walkable, the innovation district has to provide the potential for unexpected encounters, interesting shops, architectural diversity, short blocks, small green parks, and streets with trees to protect people against heat and rain. Human behavior is influenced by incentives. The time you spend walking short distances (15 to 20 minutes) instead of taking your car (5 to 10 minutes) has to be compensated by incentives that can be financial, social, aesthetic, or personal. Financial incentives refer to the price of owning and parking a car. Social incentives refer to meeting acquaintances or new people along your walks. Aesthetic incentives include visual discoveries—architectural gems, natural surroundings (parks, trees, mountains, flowers), beautiful men or women, and interesting shop windows. Personal incentives refer to the well-being and health benefits one gains from walking. Those four incentives combine to spur a walking culture among a district's residents.

PRODUCTIVE

(3) Innovation districts are productive districts. They instill a new economic dynamic in which new productive activities transform the district. Innovation districts offer new employment and creative opportunities as well as the possibility for individuals to self-actualize. In the productive layer there are three important elements that have to be present: knowledge-intensive activities, diversity- and/or cluster-based development approach, and entrepreneurship.

Innovation districts are hubs for knowledge-intensive companies. Innovation districts are privileged areas for the location of knowledge-intensive activities. The focus on knowledge-intensive activities is perceived for urban leaders as a strategy to reorganize the economy toward a more intensive use of the urban economic fabric. As seen in chapter 1, knowledge-intensive activities have three main benefits. First, knowledge-intensive activities foster productivity and, thus, urban competitiveness. Second, knowledge-intensive activities create high-quality jobs that are highly localized. Third, knowledge-intensive activities offer urban areas a sustained economic advantage. Innovation districts that are natural habitats for knowledge-intensive companies confer three distinct competitive advantages for knowledge-intensive companies.

First, innovation districts provide knowledge-intensive companies with access to a talented pool of knowledge workers. Innovation districts serve as marketing tools for recruiting creative and innovative individuals. A location in an innovation district gives smaller innovative companies an edge in attracting and retaining the best knowledge workers. Indeed, many millennials would accept lower wages to work for a hip company and live in an exciting and funky neighborhood. In the knowledge economy, a sustained competitive advantage relies on knowledge-intensive companies' capacities to attract the best and brightest workers. There is an ongoing war for talent among the most innovative companies, as Facebook's Mark Zuckerberg points out, "Someone who is exceptional in their role is not just a little better than someone who is pretty good, they are 100 times better" (Helft, 2011). Innovative companies thrive on innovative employees. Thus, it makes sense for such companies to pay a premium to be located in innovation districts and gain access to a larger pool of talented knowledge workers.

Second, innovation districts facilitate collaboration, open innovation, and spillovers, which in turn accelerate the process of innovation. Innovation districts strengthen innovative companies' innovative capacities and, thus, reinforce their competitive advantages. Open innovation and living labs reduce transaction costs for developing and testing prototypes. Sophisticated customers in the innovation districts can give direct, unbiased feedback on new products, software, and service. Innovative companies who interact on a daily basis with entrepreneurs, artists, and knowledge workers are updated on the latest emerging technologies. More important, the colocation of knowledge-intensive companies in the same district creates a healthy competition that reinforces their innovative capacities.

Third, an innovation district provides smaller knowledge-intensive companies with an innovative legitimacy and an urban campus. Knowledge-intensive companies that locate in an innovation district signal a strong commitment to stay in the race for innovation, a signal that is particularly important for smaller companies trying to influence potential investors, clients, and suppliers. Few innovative companies can build a Googleplex corporate headquarters, but many can locate their offices in an innovation district that becomes an extension of the office. The coffee shop at the street corner serves as a meeting room, the indie cinema as a conference center, the rooftop bar as a relaxation room, and the park as the fitness center; and there are many restaurants to choose from for business lunches. Innovation districts are both playgrounds and open corporate campuses.

Innovation districts feature clusters. Michael Porter (1990; 2008; 2011) was inspired by the work of Alfred Marshall (1890), Giacomo

Becattini (1990), Piore and Sabel (1984), and the GREMI (1986) to develop the concept of clusters. Clusters differ from industrial districts in that national and local governments can affect the productive frameworks of clusters. In the cluster framework, the interaction between local institutions and individual firms is central (Belussi & Sammarra, 2009). Porter (1990) argued that in the current globalized world clusters are the critical mass that makes location important. Companies will relocate around the world within their industry's cluster. Specific urban areas may represent a specific cluster: for instance, finance is New York, Hong Kong, and London; entertainment is Los Angeles; ICT is San Francisco; oil is Houston; fashion is Milan; and country music is Nashville (Storper, 2013). Michael Porter (2008) defined clusters as "[t]he geographic concentrations of interconnected companies, specialized suppliers, service providers, firms in related industries, and associated institutions (for example, universities, standards agencies, and trade associations) in particular fields that compete but also cooperate" (p. 214).

The geographic scope of a cluster can range from a city to a network of neighboring countries. Clusters are present in large and small economies, in rural and urban areas, and at several geographic levels. Clusters occur in both advanced and developing economies, although in advanced economies they tend to be more sophisticated. Clusters vary in size, breadth, and state of development. Some clusters consist primarily of small- and medium-sized firms, whereas other clusters involve both large and small firms. Some clusters center on research universities, whereas others have no important university connections.

According to Michael Porter (2008), two fundamental elements define a cluster: interconnectedness and proximity. Indeed, firms in a cluster must be linked in some way. The links are both vertical (buying and selling chains) and horizontal (complementary products and services, the use of similar specialized inputs, and technologies or institutions, and other linkages) [Martin & Sunley, 2003]. The second element is that firms in a cluster are geographically proximate. Co-location encourages the formation of clusters and enhances the value-creating benefits of interactivity between firms (Martin & Sunley, 2003).

Agglomeration and networks emerge from those two fundamental characteristics of the cluster approach (Kresl, 2014). Agglomeration leads to positive externalities for firms that cluster together. The network creates private structures in which geographical proximity is not a relevant factor, and the network benefits the cluster in that information and knowledge are easily disseminated. Agglomeration and networks contribute to what Porter (1990) called *spillovers*, or the amplification of productivity and innovation related to clustering. Besides spillovers, another key element in Porter's cluster framework is competition. Clusters favor competitive pressure and push companies to innovate (Porter, 2008). The combination of cooperation and competition facilitates spillovers and innovations, which are the two most relevant advantages of clusters.

Moreover, clustering signals an opportunity for companies and reduces the perceived risks of entry, but clusters have costs as well as benefits. The advantages clusters claim include higher innovation, growth, and productivity; increased profitability and competitiveness; and creation of more new firms and jobs (Martin & Sunley, 2003). The potential disadvantages are technological isomorphism, labor cost inflation, inflation of land and housing costs, widening of income disparities, overspecialization, institutional and industrial lock-in, local congestion, and environmental pressure (Martin & Sunley, 2003). Clusters affect competition in three broad ways: first, by increasing the productivity of constituent firms or industries; second, by increasing their capacity for innovation and productivity growth; and third, by stimulating new business formation that supports innovation and expands the cluster (Porter, 2008).

Local governments have a role to play in the cluster framework. Policymakers have turned cluster developments into a standard policy for successful local economic development (Ketels, 2003). Most decisive policy actions are undertaken at the microeconomic level; local governments must promote the cluster's sophistication and, thus, play an indirect rather than a direct role (Porter, 2008). Cluster policies at the urban level are a fashionable concept among policy makers, urban leaders, and civil society as a whole (Kresl, 2014). However, creating a cluster from scratch is a lengthy and costly process with a high failure rate (Ketels, 2003). As a result, most local governments favor policies that offer easily perceived, short-term benefits such as subsidies, protections, and arranged mergers—the very policies that retard innovation (Porter, 2008). Instead, local governments should create pressure and challenges for companies to spur innovation. Cluster development efforts must embrace the pursuit of competitive advantage and specialization that requires strategic planning and differentiation at the urban level. Local governments should not jump on the first fad technology; all clusters can be desirable, and all offer the potential to contribute to prosperity.

Clusters can be initiated either by market forces, as in Silicon Valley, California, or by public intervention, as in Austin, Texas, both of which are part of the software cluster (Wood, Simmie, & Sennet, 2002). Public interventions can take decades before any benefits emerge, as the development of North Carolina's Research Triangle illustrates. In North Carolina, the explicit decision was made in 1959 to invest heavily in universities and research infrastructures to develop a relatively rural region of the United States (Ketels, 2003). Four decades later, the region has become a serious player in the research-dependent life sciences field (Ketels, 2003). But the development and promotion of a single cluster can represent a risky strategy. A highly specialized regional economy can easily be confronted by a structural crisis that causes turmoil, as in the case of the automobile cluster in Detroit, Michigan. Clusters are also vulnerable to the lock-in effect and to path-dependency, both of which cause them to become unresponsive to change. Local government increasingly tends to favor a diversity-based approach that does not discriminate based on industry type but rather on companies' innovative capacities. The diversity-based approach, the local policy approach that emanates from the writings of Jane Jacobs (1961), is less risky from a political standpoint and, thus, is becoming the preferred local economic development initiative.

For Jacobs (1961), a highly specialized city does not spur innovation but rather annihilates it. The most innovative cities are *entrepôt* cities in which outsiders with different backgrounds and different skills work alongside one another. Cities with diverse industries and that are open to outsiders are most likely to innovate and thrive. Cities dominated by one industry and that are closed to outsiders are likely to decline. The confrontation between new and established ways of doing things is likely to produce innovations. Empirically, this argument is confirmed by the decline of cities such as Detroit that relied only on the automobile industry led by Ford and General Motors, or Rochester, New York, that relied on the photography industry led by Eastman Kodak. The specialization of cities was endorsed to the extreme in the USRR where entire cities were built around a specific industry. Magnitogorsk, a city of half a million in the Urals, was built in the 1930s around extracting and processing iron ore (Bohlen, 1998). The once state-run company Magnitogorsk Iron and Steel Works was employing half of the city's workforce and contributed up to 40% of the city's taxes. However, the model of specialization never brought the innovative panacea that had been expected.

Municipal leaders should promote cluster development in certain industries. At the urban level, economies of agglomeration and localization are the main cluster advantages for companies. As a result, the industries requiring face-to-face transmission of knowledge will be the most successful in urban areas. These industries include fashion and design, furniture, ICT, advertising, publishing, cinema, and video games (Storper, 2013). Confined geographical spaces such as Manhattan and Hong Kong are favored because creative workers can easily encounter one another in serendipitous ways and exchange knowledge (Kresl, 2014). Urban strategies should leverage knowledge-based activities that require access to the latest thinking and trends because urban spaces provide the best structures for face-to-face transmission of knowledge.

The concept of clusters has become increasingly associated with the knowledge economy, and clusters are seen as a development tool to foster spillovers that, in turn, raise the city's innovative and productive capacity. Moreover, clusters are seen as a development tool to drive up exports and foster a thriving tradable sector, the economic drivers of a city's prosperity. The tradable sector provides highly localized jobs, local service jobs, and a sustained competitive advantage (Storper, 2013). Clusters are also a magnet for attracting investments and foreign direct investments (FDIs). Indeed, locating within a cluster can provide superior or lower-cost access to specialized inputs such as raw materials, machinery, business services, and labor as compared to the alternatives (Porter, 2008). Consequently, companies locate in a cluster to increase their capacity to innovate that triggers a self-reinforcing process. The environment creates a healthy support structure with specialized suppliers, local institutions, research centers, infrastructures, and a critical mass that attracts more companies as the visibility of the cluster grows.

In the knowledge economy, the concept of clustering complements the concept of diversity. The development of a cluster will be successful for cities provided there is a sufficient critical mass to sustain the cluster, as we will see in the next chapter. Usually, the right strategy for most cities is to promote a diverse economic base with knowledge-intensive activities. When the city has a critical mass to sustain clusters, it is recommended that the city include at least two clusters to promote a diversity-based cluster development.

Innovation districts have entrepreneurs, startups, and spinoffs. Innovation districts aim to attract, generate, and retain entrepreneurs, startups, and spinoffs. Entrepreneurship fulfills three aspects of the productive framework. First, entrepreneurs participate in so-called "creative destruction." Second, entrepreneurs accelerate the cluster's sophistication and foster new knowledge-intensive activities; entrepreneurs triggered the success of innovative clusters including Silicon Valley and Cambridge in Boston. Third, entrepreneurship has become a hip career choice and a potential solution for governments to reduce unemployment.

According to Schumpeter (2013), entrepreneurs are those who revolutionize the pattern of production and are, as a result, essential for economic development. Entrepreneurs and small firms play a fundamental role in innovation by enabling the creative destruction process for innovation and economic development (Schumpeter, 2013). Additionally, entrepreneurs and start-ups are a fundamental component of Porter's cluster theory. Indeed, an environment keen on entrepreneurship enables competition and rivalry that, in turn, fosters innovation. Innovation districts favor the formation of spinoffs and the creation of small technology companies, and that contributes to the rapid dissemination of new technologies. In the old industrial model, the creation and transfer of knowledge took place within the company (Saxenian, 1994). In the new economy, however, the fast rise and death rates of spinoffs and start-ups promote mobility, the spread of tacit knowledge, and the adoption of technologies that favor innovation. The knowledge economy favors collaboration and competition, and entrepreneurship is, consequently, a key productive element of the new economic paradigm.

Entrepreneurship has played a crucial role in the development of knowledge-intensive regions such as Silicon Valley and Cambridge, Massachusetts. Annalee Saxenian (1994) has identified entrepreneurs as being at the forefront of Silicon Valley's success. In the 1990s, the entrepreneurs of Silicon Valley were able to adapt their products to the new technological paradigm whereas Route 128 in Massachusetts, which relied heavily on government procurements from the

Department of Defense, declined as the military budget waned (Saxenian, 1994).

Universities play an important role in fostering entrepreneurship in knowledge-intensive industries. The Massachusetts Institute of Technology (MIT) and Stanford University have transformed their respective regions through the creation of high-tech spinoffs—high-growth companies that were first created in universities. At the university level, five resources are relevant to entrepreneurship: students, professors, research labs, entrepreneurship programs, and technology transfer offices (Feld, 2012). Research and technology-intensive universities, via their entrepreneurial spinoffs, have a strong impact on the U.S. economy (Roberts & Eesley, 2011). For example, if the sum of the total revenues of companies founded by MIT graduates were the GDP of a nation, it would be the 17th-largest economy in the world (Roberts & Eesley, 2011). As of 2011, MIT alumni have founded about 25,800 active companies, employing about 3.3 million people and generating annual world revenue of about $2 trillion (Roberts & Eesley, 2011). Over the years, the MIT entrepreneurial environment has attracted entrepreneurial-minded students, staff, and faculty, leading to a strong entrepreneurial feedback loop (Roberts & Eesley, 2011). The companies founded by MIT students and professors have deeply changed the district around the campus, which evolved from a derelict industrial district to a flourishing innovation zone. More than a quarter of the companies (a projected 6,900) founded by MIT scholars and alumni are headquartered in Massachusetts, mostly in

Kendall Square in Cambridge (Roberts & Eesley, 2011).

The choice of becoming an entrepreneur is now widely accepted (even in France), thanks to new attitudes and cultural norms. For instance, in HEC Paris, the top business school in France, 25% of the class of 2014 decided to become entrepreneurs in comparison with only 2% of the class of 2004 (HEC, 2015). This improved perception of entrepreneurship results from the images of the successful entrepreneurs of Silicon Valley, the increased relative instability and flexibility required in the job market, the increased unemployment rates of both unskilled workers and skilled college graduates, and the appeal of the hacker ethic in opposition to the dull corporate life. Silicon Valley's entrepreneurs consider themselves pioneers and outsiders who are experimenting with new technologies in a new region (Saxenian, 1994). The charismatic personalities of Steve Jobs, Mark Zuckerberg, and Elon Musk have become role models for many students aspiring to entrepreneurship. Peter Thiel, cofounder of PayPal, donates money to encourage students to drop out of university on the condition they create innovative start-ups. For many, lifestyle entrepreneurship offers an alternative to the regular 9 to 5 corporate job. Lifestyle entrepreneurs start businesses, not primarily for economic reward, but for the opportunity to enjoy a better lifestyle (Markantoni, Koster, & Striker, 2012). For example, most lifestyle entrepreneurs who start blogs, YouTube channels, social media websites, and so on, don't make much money, but they enjoy the social rewards. Today, it is more socially rewarding to be a blogger than a business analyst working in a bland office park. "Follow your dreams" and "Do what you love" are the mottos of the millennials.

Sharon Zukin in *Loft Living* (1989) describes how the elites who feared that mass unemployment was leading to social unrest pushed creative works as essential values for self-actualization. The precept goes like this: If you are doing something you like, you are less likely to revolt. In our time of mass unemployment and underemployment, the promotion of entrepreneurship is not only a means to spur economic growth and create jobs; it also is a social control mechanism.

Seed accelerators, start-up incubators, and venture capital companies form the necessary ecosystem to attract and retain entrepreneurs. The promotion of those companies and the creation of coworking spaces in widely diverse cities are harbingers of the elevated status of entrepreneurs as engines for growth in the new economy. Seed accelerators are particularly important in fostering a strong entrepreneurial ecosystem. The municipal organization in charge of piloting the district's transformation into an innovation district should allocate a part of its budget to establish a local not-for-profit seed accelerator modeled on successful seed accelerators such as the Y Combinator that was an early investor in Dropbox, Airbnb, and Reddit, among many other startups. Created in 2005, Y Combinator provides advice, connections, mentorships, and funding to promising and fast-growing startups. The seed accelerator works as a boot camp in which startups move to Silicon Valley for three months and pitch to investors and venture capitalists during demo day at the end of the Y Combinator accelerator program. Seed accelerators usually take between 7% to 10% equities per US $25,000 invested in a startup. The municipal organization should allocate between US $250,000 to $5,000,000 per year for five years, depending on its competencies and financial resources, which will enable the seed accelerator to potentially fund between 10 and 200 startups a year. When a successful exit occurs, the money should go back to fund new startups, thus creating an evergreen financing model. Cities should also rehabilitate historical buildings to house entrepreneurs who, by becoming residents of prestigious landmarks in central locations, automatically confer high status on entrepreneurs, which further incentivizes others to become entrepreneurs. The San Francisco Chronicle Building, for instance, is a place for coworking, attracting many kinds of entrepreneurs. The rehabilitation of the Halle Freyssinet in Paris to house 1,000 startups demonstrates the enthusiasm of local authorities to nurture and value entrepreneurs.

The globalization and adoption of ICTs have reduced transaction costs for entrepreneurs to found start-ups (Knight, 1996). The changing paradigm allows entrepreneurs to locate around the world, thanks to many countries' relaxed visa programs for entrepreneurs. International entrepreneurs are highly mobile and choose to locate where they find the best opportunities (McDougall & Oviatt, 2003; Oviatt, McDougall, & Loper, 1995). Cities such as Medellin, Colombia, and Barcelona, Spain, aim to attract born-global firms and international entrepreneurs by building specific spaces for them, such as landing platforms and residences (www.rutanmedellin.org). In the case of landing platforms, entrepreneurs become part of the startup ecosystem as soon as they plug their computers into the coworking spaces specifically designed for them.

Globalization is creating a "brain circulation" in which immigrants are returning to their countries to create startups (Saxenian, 2006). For Saxenian (2006), globalization creates mobility and favors brain circulation. Indeed, countries that suffered most from the postwar brain drain—especially Taiwan, Israel, India, and China—are those now benefitting most from international entrepreneurship (Saxenian, 2006). It follows that cities must create the innovation ecosystems and entrepreneurial environments to attract and retain international entrepreneurs.

Auerswald and Branscomb (2003) discussed the extent to which public policies can influence entrepreneurship. The progress from inventions to innovations—that is, of new technologies and patents to commercially viable products—is a complex process and a financial burden. The authors have identified an innovation or funding gap during early stage technology development (ESTD) that prevents ideas from becoming commercially viable. The funding gap can be crossed through seed venture funding, government R&D programs, and the participation of angel investors (Branscomb, 2003). Auerswald and Branscomb (2003) highlighted opportunities for governments—and in more and more cases, for cities—to fund start-ups to break bottlenecks that cause good ideas to never bridge the ESTD.

Local governments push entrepreneurship because it is also a means to foster job creation and to lower endemic unemployment rates. Entrepreneurship is one of the few levers that local governments can influence to reduce unemployment. In the European Union, youth unemployment has reached critical levels to the extent that it threatens the future standard of living of its citizens. As of the second quarter of 2014, there were 5 million unemployed young people between 18 and 25, representing an unemployment rate of 21.7% (European Commission, 2015). The situation is particularly dire for Mediterranean countries where youth unemployment is as high as 50% in Spain and Greece, 40% in Italy and Portugal, and 25% in France (European Commission, 2015). More troubling is that 7.5 million young Europeans are not involved in employment, education, or other training (the so-called NEETs). Without a doubt, the young generation will be a sacrificed generation that will have lower standards of living than that of their parents. In our highly competitive labor markets, the unemployed of today will be the unemployable of tomorrow. According to Tapan Munroe (2010), startups were the largest job creators during the last decade in the United States. Indeed, while larger corporations have instituted extensive downsizing agendas, job creation and economic growth are coming from startups and the entrepreneurs who initiate them (Mazzarol, Volery, Doss, & Thein, 1999). Additionally, policy initiatives to promote entrepreneurship are easy to implement and, potentially, can be highly rewarding in terms of job creation, innovation, and economic growth.

COLLABORATIVE

(4) The collaborative layer rests on five pillars: the triple-helix model of innovation, living labs, open innovation, universities, and spaces for collaboration. Among those five pillars: the spaces for collaboration are a distinctive feature of innovation districts. The five pillars of the innovation district's collaborative layer are fostered by proximity and tacit knowledge. The collaborative layer spurs proximity and the spread of tacit knowledge, which accelerate collaboration and hence the process of innovation.

Innovation districts are planned around one or more universities. Universities have a central function in fostering innovation. Traditionally, universities have focused on training students and producing basic and applied knowledge. However, in the past decade the changing role of universities has evolved into wealth creation as the direct result of reduced public spending for education in developed economies (OECD, 1998). Consequently, universities have adapted to deliver value and function more productively in the economy by seeking new capabilities and commercializing innovation (Youtie & Shapira, 2008). Indeed, universities are not only generating basic and applied knowledge and educating the labor force but are also supporting entrepreneurial ecosystems, facilitating spinoffs, and developing new ventures. The role of universities has evolved from being knowledge storehouses to knowledge factories to knowledge hubs (Youtie & Shapira, 2008). The OECD (1998) emphasizes that universities need to be managed and compete as private institutions. Universities must generate basic and applied knowledge that are useful and in line with local economic strategies. The capacities and specific training developed by universities must match the specific market's needs. As pointed out by Castells and Hall (1994), for universities to play a role in the information-based economy, they need to have industry linkages. This new paradigm for universities obliges them to adapt to the local demand and guide students to specific careers paths. In this new model, students are operational and productive as soon as they graduate, companies easily have access to the specific skills in demand, and universities can secure private funding to upgrade and attract faculty and students. In this new paradigm, universities are assumed to stimulate technological spillovers, research productivity, patenting, licensing, foster entrepreneurship, and produce spinoffs (Siegel, Westhead, & Wright, 2003).

Annalee Saxenian (1994), in her influential book *Regional Advantage: Culture and Competition in Silicon Valley and Route 128* highlights the positive role of academic institutions in the economic success of those two knowledge hubs. Indeed, the MIT and Stanford played a critical role in the development of the two regions. The successful knowledge ecosystems that have emerged from MIT and Stanford have influenced urban policy makers around the world to replicate and to develop knowledge ecosystems from regional universities.

While entrepreneurs, innovative ventures, and startups were locating in Silicon Valley, large corporations were locating in Route 128, attracted to government procurements from the Department of Defense. Silicon Valley largely relied on private consumption, and Route 128 mostly relied on public procurements. Route 128 was a successful innovation ecosystem in the 70s at the peak of the Cold War, while Silicon Valley became a thriving innovation ecosystem in the 90s and has been ever since. Government procurements and MIT fostered the development of Route 128, and Silicon Valley emerged from Stanford and its links to private companies. It follows that the public sector can drive the development of knowledge hubs, but the private sector is needed to sustain them. For instance, the emergence of Austin as an innovation hub arose from expansion of research at the University of Texas, which was encouraged by the State of Texas, local companies, and federal funds (Etzkowitz & Leydesdorff, 2000). Stanford has played a critical role in the development of Silicon Valley. The university has been, without doubt, the catalyst of the valley's remarkable success. Stanford is located in the Santa Clara Valley, which was known for its apricot and prune orchards and, until the early 1970s, a popular name for the Santa Clara Valley was the Valley of the Heart's Delight, not Silicon Valley (Gibbons, 2000). Silicon Valley would have been markedly different today without Stanford and the dedication of its dean, Frederick Terman, who can be credited as the founding father of Silicon Valley. In the late 1930s, Terman was frustrated with the lack of jobs for graduates of Stanford's electrical Engineering Department, and that led him to energetically encourage entrepreneurship (Gibbons, 2000). Terman was an angel investor in Hewlett-Packard (incorporated in 1939), providing $500 in seed capital. Silicon Valley gradually grew around Stanford Research Park, which was founded in 1951 when Terman developed and leased university lands for start-ups founded by Stanford graduates (Gibbons, 2000). Today, Silicon Valley is the most innovative region in the world.

Innovation districts use the triple helix model of innovation. Loet Leydesdorff and Henry Etzkowitz (1996) provide a model in which university-industry-government cooperate to spur innovation. In their model, universities play an enhanced role in that universities provide the necessary knowledge to generate innovation (Etzkowitz & Leydesdorff, 2000). In the 1990s, the role of universities has considerably changed (OECD, 1998). The triple helix model for innovation emerged from the evolving role of universities, the specific nature of knowledge hubs such as Silicon Valley or Route 128, and the new functions of governments and institutions. In the 1990s, developed economies and newly industrialized economies have formulated innovation strategies based upon the deliberate elaboration of academic-industry relations through reflexive Science and Technologies policies (Leydesdorff & Etzkowitz, 1996). The new knowledge-based economic paradigm has made the distinction between laissez-faire and active-state intervention obsolete; governments and public institutions must become enablers and facilitators. In Saxenian's (1994) analysis on Route 128 and Silicon Valley, governments can drive the creation of knowledge hubs but only the private sector can maintain them in the long run. Policies must support network-based industrial systems and serve as catalysts by stimulating and coordinating cooperation among firms and between private companies and the public sector (Saxenian, 1994). Rather than being orchestrated as top-down intervention or bureaucratic guidance, policy initiatives should evolve as interested local parties exchange information, negotiate, and collaborate (Saxenian, 1994).

Leydesdorff and Etzkowitz (1996) conceptualized the triple helix model of innovation in which industry cooperates with government and universities to foster innovation and create wealth. The triple helix's objective is to achieve a sustainable innovative ecosystem involving university spin-off firms, trilateral initiatives for knowledge-based economic development, strategic alliances among firms (large and small, operating in different areas, and with different technologies), government laboratories, and academic research groups (Etzkowitz & Leydesdorff, 2000). These arrangements are often encouraged but not controlled by governments, whether through new rules of the game such as the Bayh-Dole Act that encourages researchers to commercialize products, or through direct or indirect financial assistance (Etzkowitz & Leydesdorff, 2000). In the triple helix model, the three spheres are not defined institutionally; each assumes the role of the other two due to the constant interactions through a number of institutions such as industrial liaison, technology transfer, and contract offices (Leydesdorff & Etzkowitz, 1998). The triple helix model of university-industry-government relations can be generalized from "a neo-institutional model of networks of relations to a neo-evolutionary model of how three selected environments operate upon one another" (Leydesdorff & Meyer, 2008).

In the triple helix model of innovation, each actor plays a different role at each stage of business growth. The support of the university and government are especially important in the first stage of creation and implementation; however, during the later stages of growth and maturity, the private sector has to create networks and linkages between the companies and the different players (Garriga, Sánchez, & Solé Parellada, 2011). The linear model, expressed in terms of market pull or technology push, is insufficient to induce the transfer of knowledge and technology. The triple helix model incorporates the different product life and innovation cycles to induce a transfer of knowledge and technology. Science parks are incorporating the triple helix. The traditional double helices in science parks of industry-government or university-industry collaborations have expanded to incorporate the triple helix of university-industry-government relations. While the double helices innovation model was adequate to Greenfield science parks, cities are the best entities to receive and implement the triple helix model. The suburban technology parks are replaced by urban science parks—a dense infrastructure of R&D clusters, universities, agencies to support innovation, hybrid organizations, and networks that encompass elements drawn from academia, industry, and government (Etzkowitz, Solé, & Piqué, 2010).

Open innovation and living labs play a key role in innovation districts. Innovation districts are designed on the quadruple helix model of innovation. In this model industry, government, universities, and civil society unite to build a well-configured innovation ecosystem for the knowledge economy and society at large (Carayannis & Campbell, 2009). Chesbrough (2003) describes an innovation paradigm shift from a closed to an open model (Cherbrough & Crowther, 2006). For the authors, companies gain a competitive advantage from inbound open innovation, which refers to the practice of leveraging the discoveries of others (Cherbrough & Crowther, 2006). The notion that companies can rely solely on their internal R&D capacities is outdated. Companies should force themselves to learn from and collaborate with others to sustain their competitive advantages. To the concept of inbound open innovation the authors add the concept of outbound open innovation, suggesting that "rather than relying entirely on internal paths to market, companies can look for external organizations with business models that are better suited to commercialize a given technology" (Cherbrough & Crowther, 2006).

Living labs are the tools used to spur open innovation. In livings labs end-users participate in the conception of products by testing and improving prototypes. Companies located in innovation districts benefit from a large pool of sophisticated consumers eager to participate in developing new products through living and urban labs. As a result, innovative companies can find out in real time how popular their products will be.

Innovation districts have spaces for collaboration. The combination of proximity, tacit knowledge, and networks is central to the process of innovation and is one of the key elements of the success of knowledge-intensive clusters such as Silicon Valley, Silicon Alley, Cambridge (MA and UK), and so on. The creation of spaces for collaboration in innovation districts aims to accelerate the proximity, tacit knowledge, and networks that are primary for innovation and, thus, accelerate the process of innovation. The spaces for collaboration can be informal: coffee shops, bars, parks, or restaurants. In Silicon Valley in the 1970s and 1980s, the most famous informal spaces—such as Walker's Wagon Wheel Bar and Grill in Mountain View—have probably disseminated more ideas than conventional seminars (Castells, 2011). Formal spaces for collaboration are created specifically to foster collaboration among knowledge-intensive companies and can take the form of coworking spaces, libraries, landing platforms, fab labs, hackerspaces, shared laboratories, and so on. According to the Fab Foundation, a fab lab is a technical prototyping platform for innovation and invention that stimulates local entrepreneurship. Fab labs are spaces where members share access to state-of-the-art equipment such as 3D printers, laser cutters, and numerical control machines. The first fab lab was created at MIT, which, through the Fab Foundation, provides guidelines and advice on how to establish a fab lab anywhere. There are approximately

450 fab labs in cities around the world (http://www.fabfoundation.org/). One of the most advanced spaces for collaboration is the MediaTic building in Barcelona where entrepreneurs, seed accelerators, incubators, research centers, venture capitalists, consultants, lawyers, seed capital companies, public institutions, and private companies work in the same landmark building at the heart of Barcelona's innovation district.

Innovation districts foster proximity. The triple helix model of innovation aims to promote the occurrence of knowledge spillovers that, in turn, can lead to innovation. Proximity is also a great catalyst to stimulate knowledge spillovers (Fisher, 2006). Knowledge spillovers are positive externalities exchanged among producers and/or users of innovation that are essential to the city's innovative capacity (Fisher, 2006). The spillovers provide what Alfred Marshall (1920) referred to "as something in the air" that favors the innovative capacity of an industrial district. Proximity was critical to the success of innovative regions like Silicon Valley or spontaneous innovation districts like the Silicon Sentier in Paris because proximity favors the diffusion of tacit knowledge and the learning of new skills. Geographic proximity also played an important role in the development of Silicon Valley because proximity accelerates innovation to the extent that companies located close to sophisticated potential customers have an enhanced product development innovative capacity (Saxenian, 1994). While Silicon Valley has relative higher costs than neighboring regions, proximity creates networks that are essential to the innovative capacities of the companies located in the region. Geographic proximity allows firms to monitor emerging technologies, to adapt to market change, and to be updated on any technological breakthrough (Saxenian, 1994). Proximity facilitates the frequent face-to-face communications needed for successful collaboration while intensifying competition. Proximity in Silicon Valley, marked by cognitive, geographical, organizational, and network proximity, is a model difficult to replicate in emerging knowledge hubs (Saxenian, 1994).

In the late 1990s Internet startups began to locate in the second arrondissement of Paris, later dubbed Silicon Sentier (Vicente et al., 2007). Silicon Sentier, which emerged independently as Paris' Internet hub with more than 300 Internet companies, did not have any kind of government planning (Vicente et al., 2007). Proximity works as a signaling for entrepreneurs to locate their startups in the Silicon Sentier. In 1997 Yahoo played the role of a fashion leader and contributed to the location signal that "provided new entrants with the legitimacy they did not have due to their recent creation" (Suire & Vicente, 2009). Thus, fashion leaders can influence the trajectories of collective choices in the early stages of the clustering process by reducing uncertainty among location alternatives, increasing legitimacy, finding partners, having access to external knowledge, and enjoying knowledge spillovers (Suire & Vicente, 2009). Consequently, proximity provides a strong motive for mimetic interactions and can account for the emergence of collective behaviors (Suire & Vicente, 2009).

Gilly and Torre (2000) divide proximity into three separate concepts: geographical, organizational, and institutional. Boschma (2005) develops the concept of cognitive proximity as a relevant addition to the Gilly and Torre (2000) framework. Geographical proximity, which refers to the geographic distance that separates companies and individuals (Gilly & Torre, 2000), is easily quantifiable, specifically through transport and telecommunication metrics.

Organizational proximity refers to the degree of separation or closeness between individuals and/or organizations in a strictly economic sense (Gilly & Torre, 2000). Organizational proximity is further defined between adherence and similarity logics. Adherence logic refers to the degree and intensity of direct interactions between agents; similarity logic refers to specific categories into which people are assigned (Gilly & Torre, 2000).

Institutional proximity refers to the rule of the game—the fact that agents share the same space of representation and face the same incentives and constraints in the legal and economic framework (Gilly & Torre, 2000). Institutional proximity adds a collective dimension among the agents when interacting. Boschma (2005) identifies cognitive proximity as a strong driver to spur the innovative capacity of a region.

Cognitive proximity refers to the capacity of individuals to think alike. However, strong cognitive proximity can obstruct innovative endeavors instead, thus favoring the locked-in through excessive

92

conformism (Boschma, 2005). For Florida (2002), open-minded cognitive proximity is essential to the process of innovation because diversity, tolerance, and different cognitive styles stimulate new ideas and thinking styles.

Glaeser and Maré (1994) have shown that wages are 32% higher within cities than outside metropolitan areas. The authors demonstrate that the urban wage premium comes from specific urban externalities that enhance workers' productivity (Glaeser & Maré, 1994). Indeed, cities enhance learning and general skill acquisition due to the frequent interactions among workers and the diffusion of tacit knowledge. Workers are acquiring more skills in dense environments through numerous interactions and learning possibilities (Glaeser & Maré, 1994). As a result, proximity favors learning and skills development that, in turn, improves productivity and innovation.

Thomas Allen (1984) has studied extensively the organization of innovation. Proximity matters in innovation to the extent that researchers in an R&D laboratory interact most with those located closest to them. Allen (1984) shows that, in order to maximize contact among employees, the most valuable staff members should be seated at the center of the room. Interactions among diverse firms should be promoted in order to foster complementary knowledge (Suire, & Vicente, 2009). Networks should not only focus on interactions among proximate actors, but they should also operate at the global, national, regional, and urban levels, gathering knowledge via social interaction through soft networks (Malecki, 2002).

Innovation districts promote face-to-face interactions. Proximity promotes the spread of tacit knowledge and the intensification of face-to-face interactions. The ICT and globalization have transformed the ways in which information and knowledge are produced, stored, and diffused. These transformations have accelerated the codification of knowledge and modified the balance between codified and tacit knowledge (Morgan, 2004). While codified knowledge is easily accessible around the world at any time, tacit knowledge is highly localized. The concept of death of geography can apply to codified knowledge but is not applicable to tacit knowledge. It is unlikely that ICT will ever become a surrogate for geographic space because the nuances of body language and face-to-face communication convey as much, if not more, than verbal communication (Morgan, 2004). The more easily codified knowledge can be transferred, the more valuable tacit knowledge becomes (Pinch, Henry, Jenkins, & Tallman, 2003). Thus, space and proximity have become much more relevant due to the importance of tacit knowledge and its association with innovation.

Tacit knowledge is central to the process of innovation. Tacit knowledge is opposed to explicit or codified knowledge, a formalized knowledge that can be transferred around the world in various forms in a standardized manner through technical blueprints and operating manuals (Morgan, 2004). Tacit knowledge, however, refers to the knowledge that is interpretative and includes a high degree of uncertainty. Tacit knowledge can take many forms—skills and competencies, shared beliefs, and modes of interpretation—that are specific to individuals or to groups of cooperating individuals (Fisher, 2006). Michel Polanyi captures the essence of tacit knowledge: "[W]e can know more than we can tell" (Polanyi, 1966). As a result, tacit knowledge has a social and spatial significance in learning and innovation. At the social level, tacit capabilities such as teamwork skills and organizational routines constitute the core competences of firms. At the spatial level tacit knowledge is person-embodied, context-dependent and, as a result, location-dependent. Tacit knowledge is one of the elements that explain the clustering of knowledge-intensive activities in specific locations (Lever, 2002; Morgan, 2004).

Knowledge of various types—tacit, codified, scientific, technological, cultural, aesthetic, expressive, and symbolic—is crucial for sustaining economic competitiveness (Pinch et al., 2003). Tacit knowledge is associated with superior ways of designing, manufacturing, and assembling products or delivering services that are embedded in a local context and difficult to transfer (Pinch et al., 2003). Trust, common knowledge, culture, values, and cooperation—all of which favor the spread of tacit knowledge—are more likely to develop where the participants expect to meet again (Morgan, 2004; Pinch et al., 2003). As a result, agglomerations may, over time, develop a cluster-specific form of architectural knowledge that facilitates the rapid dissemination of knowledge throughout the location by increasing the learning capacity of proximate firms and conferring cluster-specific competitive advantages (Pinch et al., 2003).

Tacit knowledge is believed to be one of the key elements behind Silicon Valley's success (Saxenian, 1994). While Silicon Valley and Route 128 were viewed as industrial counterparts located on opposite coasts in the 1980s, Silicon Valley flourished in the 1990s and Route 128 declined. Silicon Valley's success is attributed to the collective identity of its entrepreneurs and top workers. Indeed, all were white men, most were in their early twenties, many had studied engineering at Stanford or MIT, and most had no industrial experience (Saxenian, 1994). None had roots in the region; many had grown up in small towns in the Midwest and shared a mutual distrust for the establishment and East Coast institutions (Saxenian, 1994). Geographic proximity promoted the repeated interaction and mutual trust needed to sustain collaboration and the diffusion of tacit knowledge (Saxenian, 1994). Pervasive informal conversations served as a source of up-to-date information about competitors, customers, markets, and technologies (Saxenian, 1994). The high turnover rate among employees resulting from the high failure rate of startups tended to reinforce the value of personal relationships and networks (Saxenian, 1994). The business culture encouraged intense involvement among the Silicon Valley workforce and emphasized knowledge diffusion from the lowliest technicians to senior management (Saxenian, 1994). Knowledge diffusion between individuals and regional institutions such as universities, trade associations, business organizations and consultancies, venture capital firms, meetings, trade shows, conferences, seminars, and social activities was essential for diffusing tacit knowledge throughout the strata of Silicon Valley.

Spatial clustering alone does not create mutually beneficial interdependencies; the diffusion of tacit knowledge does. Moreover, the propensity for innovative activities to cluster spatially will be strongest during the early stages of innovation when tacit knowledge and experience are the most important success factors (Simmie, 2013). Tacit knowledge is embedded in people, not in information systems (Fisher, 2006). Tacit knowledge also depends on the absorptive capacity of individuals, firms, industries, and cities. Absorptive capacity refers to the ability of "an individual, firm, industry, or city to acquire, assimilate, adapt, and apply new knowledge" (Ricken & Malcotsis, 2011; Tallman, Jenkins, Henry, & Pinch, 2004). The success of Silicon Valley is due partly to the social embeddedness of the economic activity. Granovetter (1973) showed that networks with weak ties and that are "characterized by pluralistic and open-ended building strategies in which actors cultivate more extensive sets of links" are more likely to produce innovation than strong ties among a limited number of like-minded people. Certain kinds of highly embedded social networks can even hinder innovation and create path-dependency where groupthink prevents change. The social interactions and repeated contacts of actors embedded within a regional context create specific social features like habits, conventions, norms, and economic activity behaviors. Trust is one of the elements of embeddedness that facilitates tacit knowledge diffusion. At the level of the city, the combination of geographic proximity and tacit knowledge can create an embedded path dependency that will, in turn, shape a collective identity (Simmie, 2013). Industrial districts are characterized by a strong propensity toward incremental innovations favored by interaction and imitation among the different stakeholders (Belussi & Sedita, 2010). At the district level many endogenous social effects influence individuals including conformity, imitation, and contagion. Innovation spurs innovation in the sense that endogenous social effects pressure individuals to innovate when others are innovating. Endogenous social effects were strong motivators for the diffusion of an innovative culture in Silicon Valley and, as we have seen, in the Silicon Sentier (Saxenian, 1994; Suire & Vicente, 2009). Informational cascades and observational learning affect the way people behave and conform to specific regional norms, which can explain why some regions diffuse tacit knowledge more effectively than others (Manski, 2000). However, radical innovations are more likely to occur along weak, spatially distributed ties (Belussi & Sedita, 2010; Granovetter, 1973). Distance interactions are explained by the search for new capabilities and the need to form alliances to create new competencies, discover new knowledge, and innovate (Belussi & Sedita, 2010). Face-to-face encounters are the most efficient form of tacit knowledge diffusion because they provide a depth and rate of feedback impossible through other forms of communication (Storper, 2013).

The importance of physical proximity depends on the degree of tacitness involved (Morgan, 2004). Cities have to be designed to promote face-to-face contact and the spread of tacit knowledge in order to better compete in the knowledge economy (Lever, 2002). Cities with an innovative ecosystem that promotes person-to-person contacts will have an improved innovative capacity (Lever, 2002). According to Lever (2002), tacit knowledge is responsible for the spatial concentration of innovations in a small number of highly connected cities.

Innovation districts create networks. Networks promote face-to-face interactions and reinforce cognitive proximity. Social networks have been crucial to the growth of Silicon Valley and, for that matter, other successful innovative milieus (Castilla, Hwang, Granovetter, & Granovetter, 2000). As defined by Castilla et al. (2000), a social network can be defined as "a set of nodes or actors (persons or organizations) linked by social relationships or ties of a specified type. A tie or relation between two actors has both strength and content." The content might include information, advice, friendship, shared interest, or membership enhanced by some level of trust. Innovation districts should favor the creation of such networks, directly or indirectly. Innovation districts could, for instance, promote events to showcase new products or introduce startups that have recently located in the district. Innovation districts could also rent at a very low rate to associations, hackers, and computer clubs to generate the creation of bottom-up networks.

Weak networks also favor the spread of new knowledge. As demonstrated by Granovetter (1973), recruitments often occur not through close friends but through weak networks. Weak networks favor the acquisition of knowledge because its members have heterogeneous backgrounds and experiences, while members of strong networks have homogenous backgrounds and experiences. In innovation districts, weak and strong networks have equal importance. Weak networks serve as the acquisition of knowledge and ideas, while strong network facilitate the conversion of such ideas into innovations. Silicon Valley abounds with both weak and strong networks; in the late 1970s, for instance, the Homebrew Computer Club, an association of computer hobbyists, was influential in spreading new ideas and new products. It is where Steve Wozniak learned about new ideas and where Steve Jobs and Wozniak first introduced the Apple I computer to potential customers.

CREATIVE

(5) The creative layer is the combination of two popular theories: that of the creative class and that of the creative city. The objectives of the creative layer are threefold: (a) to become a transformative force for the inhabitants of the district; (b) to attract, retain, and produce creative and innovative individuals; (c) to spur the development of new activities and creative endeavors. The creative layer makes the innovation districts open to outsiders, weirdos, people with esoteric passions, and minorities. There is a common drive to experiment

and share new ideas. The inhabitants of the districts are opposed the established order and empowered by a pioneer spirit to   innovate.

Innovation districts are attractive places for the creative class and knowledge workers. Florida (2002) popularized the concept of the "creative class." For him, the capacity of a city to innovate and to be successful in the knowledge economy depends on the size of its creative class. The post-Fordist economy relies on knowledge, information, creativity, design, and symbolic values (Bontje & Musterd, 2009). Human capital is at the center of the knowledge economy to the extent that both dealing with complex information and coming up with bright ideas define the success of a regional economy (Bontje & Musterd, 2009). As a result, the competition for skilled workers among developed countries is intense. Countries such as the United States and Canada that depend on foreign talent might be threatened by such competition (Mahroum, 2000). Urban policymakers brand their cities as vibrant centers of creativity and knowledge to attract the creative class (Bontje & Musterd, 2009). Florida's (2002) perspective has a significant influence on urban policymakers to the extent that mayors around the world are designing economic development plans around "luring gay twenty-five-year-olds to their cities" (Storper, 2013). In Germany, for example, the mayor of Berlin has hyped his city as "poor, but sexy" (Storper, 2013). According to Florida (2002), cities have become a central competitive element of our time because their success or decline depends on their abilities to attract and retain the creative class.

Florida (2002) believes that creativity and creative talents improve the innovative capacity of cities. The access to talented and creative individuals is to "modern business what the access to coal and iron ore were to steel making" (Florida, 2002, p. 8). The creative class refers to a wide range of workers who take part in the creative process and range from poets to business entrepreneurs and scientists. The creative class is divided between the super-creative core and the creative professionals; they comprise around 30% of the US workforce and are growing fast (Florida, 2002). According to Florida (2002), while human capital reflects richer places, the creative class makes a place more productive and innovative. Creativity is the capacity to discover new applications from knowledge and has for outcome, innovation. Hall (1998) maintains that the most innovative cities are those most attractive to outsiders and highly skilled immigrants who are the cornerstones of urban development. Creative cities are cosmopolitan in that they renew themselves with the continuous addition of creative individuals (Hall, 1998). Cities that have been successful trading, cultural, and creative centers can be expected to perform better and adapt to the knowledge economy more successfully than cities that specialized in mass production (Bontje & Musterd, 2009).

At the urban level, the most important factor of production for knowledge-intensive companies is a highly educated and trained workforce. Audretsch (1998) has shown that concentrations of such workers are limited to a few core metropolitan regions, and the limited number of labor markets that provide suitable jobs for knowledge workers has a strong effect on the location of innovative activities. Knowledge workers tend to stay in a few regional labor markets, which increase the tendency of innovative activities to cluster in the same region (Audretsch & Feldman, 1996). As a result, urban leaders are designing policies to attract knowledge workers to their cities by promoting, for instance, a higher quality of life (Speck, 2013). According to Florida (2002), young people, especially millennials, will not even consider taking jobs in certain cities or regions, instead prioritizing a lifestyle that reinforces their own identities as creative people (Florida, 2002). Millennials want to be where the action is; they want to be part of something bigger than themselves. Millennials create their own identities according to where they live. A zip code not only serves as a status symbol; it also evokes a unique way of living. According to scholars of the creative city such as Richard Florida (2002) and Charles Landry (2008), people first decide to locate in a city and then look for jobs. Storper (2013) compares attracting skilled workers to a chicken-and-egg situation, arguing that although individuals and households do make a choice about where to locate, the choice is the egg, with the chicken being the location of jobs and opportunities to earn income. According to Storper (2013), "The geography of production drives the geography of urban development today, just as it has in the past" (p. 28).

For urban policymakers, millennials are the prized professionals to attract to sustain a competitive advantage (Cortright, 2005). Millennials are highly mobile, childless, entrepreneurial, creative, connected, and highly educated (Cortright, 2005; Florida, 2002). In 1970, half of all households included children, but of the 101 million new households expected to form between 2012 and 2025, 88% are projected to be childless (Speck, 2013). It follows that cities will have to change the way they are designed to remain attractive places for millennials to live. By 2000, 25- to 34-year-old adults were 30% more likely than other metropolitan residents to reside in close-in neighborhoods, which are defined as being around three miles from a city's central business district (CBD) [Cortright, 2005]. Urban policymakers are targeting millennials because their generation is the one most inclined to relocate.

The quality of the place is, Florida (2002) argues, what attracts the creative class to locate to a specific city. The quality of the place refers to the unique set of characteristics that defines a place and makes it attractive. The quality of the place has three dimensions: what is there, who is there, and what is going on. "What is there" refers to "the combination of the built environment and the natural environment" that favors the pursuit of creative lives (Florida, 2002, p. 274). "Who is there" refers to the "diverse kinds of people, the interaction, and the possibility to have a fulfilling community life to virtually everyone" (Florida, 2002, p. 274). "What is going on" refers to the "vibrancy of street life, café culture, arts, music, and people engaging in active, exciting, creative endeavors" (Florida, 2002, p. 281). The urban attributes the creative class most values are social and cultural amenities, the street-level scene, a sense of anonymity, nightlife, friendliness, and natural and physical beauty (Florida, 2002). Urban areas with a strong quality of place will attract knowledge workers that, in turn, will attract startups to locate in those urban areas. Downtowns have higher quality of place than suburban areas. According to Florida (2002), the downtown districts of Silicon Valley, New York City, and similar locations are thriving because of their higher quality of place.

Knowledge workers, millennials, and creative workers want to live in cities that are diverse and interesting. The weirder and more tolerant a place is, the more attractive it becomes to creative workers (Feld, 2012). The city slogan for Austin, Texas, is "Keep Austin Weird," a catchphrase that aims to appeal to and promote small businesses. Worpole and Greenhalgh (1999) suggest that the cultural diversity and intensity of a place can foster the urban creative potential of individuals. Regions and cities with important cultural agglomeration economies have a superior position for attracting and retaining innovators and brainworkers (Boschma & Lambooy, 1998). Members of the creative class do not define themselves by their economic capital but rather by their cultural capital as expressed in pioneering decisions to take up permanent residence in downtown areas once considered lower status, such as downtown Manchester, England, or Brooklyn in New York City (Allen, 2007). Openness and tolerance are crucial elements that are more likely to be found in cosmopolitan cities (Hall, 2004). Fujita et al. (2001) and Jacobs (1969) stress the importance of a heterogeneous labor force in terms of skills and experiences and the constant flow of new skills to foster innovation. For them, diversity is innovation, provided that individuals possess enough skills.

Glaeser, Scheinkman, and Shleifer (1995) examined the relationship between urban characteristics and urban growth from 1960 to 1990 in US metropolitan areas. The authors found that population growth has varied widely from city to city. In another study, Glaeser and Saiz (2003) found that between 1980 and 2000 the population of metropolitan areas in which less than 10% of adults had college degrees grew by an average of 13%. Conversely, the population of metropolitan areas in which more than 25% of adults had college degrees grew by an average of 45% (Glaeser & Saiz, 2003).

Unlike countries, cities are open economies that include important movements of capital, labor, and ideas (Glaeser et al., 1995). Aside from climate, the most significant variable to explain the divergence between cities is the initial education level of the population (Glaeser & Saiz, 2003; Glaeser et al., 1995). The divergence suggests that an educated population provides cities with the capacity to adapt their activities in response to negative economic shocks and to facilitate the emergence of innovative activities. Demand for living in high-skill cities is increasing because people learn faster in high-skill cities and are more productive, which contributes to higher wages in cities and creates a positive feedback loop that attracts more skilled labor (Glaeser, 1998; Glaeser & Saiz, 2003).

Innovation districts are creative. The creative city emerged in the late 1980s as an aspirational concept to solve urban problems (Landry, 2008). It draws from the popular concept that the creative economy can yield endless increasing returns and lead to urban prosperity and competitiveness (Howkins, 2002; Landry, 2008). The success of the creative city concept is due to the convergence between cultural spheres and economic development (Scott, 1997). Human culture is subject to commodification, and cities are not exempt from this rule; nevertheless, place, culture, and economy are highly symbiotic (Scott, 1997). The creative city's objective is twofold: it aims to regenerate declining urban areas and to create new urban creative industries. Since the 1980s cultural quarters have become a tool for urban regeneration to offset economic restructuring and related social and environmental degradation of declining cities (Porter & Barber, 2007). Deindustrialization, the highly localized nature of creative industries, and the rise of the experience economy contributed to this shift in urban development (Ashworth & Voogd, 1990; Pine & Gilmore, 1998).

Landry (2008) lists the factors that urban innovators must leverage to build their versions of the creative city. First, the city should have the right urban leaders to instill change; second, the city should have a diverse, tolerant, mixed, and skilled workforce; third, the organizational culture should be flexible and fit the new necessities of the creative economy; fourth, the city should have a strong local identity; fifth, public spaces should be numerous, mixed, and inclusive; and sixth, networks and associative structures should be extensive within and between organizations at the urban, national, and international levels.

For Florida (2002) and Landry (2008), cities compete for skilled and creative workers through the quality of their amenities, services, public realms, and entertainment. The rise of the creative economy means that wealth relies on individuals' creativity (Howkins, 2002). The clustering of talents, skills, and supporting infrastructure is central to the creative economy and creative milieu (Landry, 2008), and the creative city must provide the urban assets to foster a creative ecosystem. In the creative economy communication, collaboration, and partnership should be stimulated at the urban level (Landry, 2008).

According to Florida (2002), Silicon Valley thrives because of the open, different, and supportive environment it offers the creative class. Senior professionals in Silicon Valley cite "the Santa Clara Valley as a place to live and work" as being extremely important to the region's transformation into a knowledge hub (Gibbons, 2000). In Silicon Valley some companies decide to locate themselves within a ten-minute commute of Stanford University's landmark, Hoover tower. Although an expensive location, the companies believe the interactions between their employees, high-quality students, academics, and the opportunity to recruit talented graduates make their choice a no-brainer (Gibbons, 2000). Creative individuals do not move for traditional reasons. They seek "abundant high-quality amenities and experiences, an openness to diversity of all kinds, and above all else the opportunity to validate their identities as creative people" (Florida, 2002). Those specific amenities, however, exist only in a small subset of cities. For instance, in the United States the creative clusters are concentrated in Los Angeles, San Francisco, and New York City (Scott, 1997).

The main challenge for urban leaders when designing their city's innovation district is to find the inherent and unique creative advantage that their city possesses. The city not only has to have sufficient cultural amenities but also a unique vibe. More importantly, the uniqueness of the city must be something that is highly valued by the creative class, such as a unique coffee culture, a design or artistic city, or a city of beautiful and friendly people (Medellin in Colombia, for instance). The city's uniqueness must be enhanced, played with, and smartly communicated. It will find an audience. Urban leaders, especially in Europe, have been stuck in old paradigms, which is reflected in how their cities communicate. Every city in Europe emphasizes in its promotional "Invest in (City X)" leaflets that they are, unsurprisingly, a gateway to other cities, or that they are centrally located.

Landry (2008) defines the creative milieu as an atmosphere that fosters the creative economy, much like GREMI's (1986) innovative milieu. The creative milieu is "a place either a cluster of buildings, a part of a city, a city as a whole or a region that contains the necessary preconditions in terms of hard and soft infrastructure to generate a flow of ideas and inventions" (Landry, 2008, p.133).

The creative milieu includes a critical mass of creative individuals that generates new ideas through tacit knowledge. Hard infrastructures include research institutes, universities, cultural facilities, and "third places" (Oldenburg, 1989) as well as support services such as transport, health care, and amenities (Landry, 2008). Soft infrastructure is the system of associative structures and social networks, connections, and human interactions that encourages the flow of ideas between individuals and institutions (Landry, 2008). A culture of collaborative competition is necessary for the creative milieu to thrive (Landry, 2008).

Urban development policies are beginning to focus on attracting both the creative class and skilled workers, reflecting the paradigm shift from chasing companies to chasing knowledge workers. When he was mayor of New York City, Michael Bloomberg decided that economic policy should be based on providing businesses with appropriate space, infrastructure, talent, quality of life, and living conditions that, rather than focusing on financial incentives to lure large corporations, would enable startups and innovative companies to gain a unique economic value from being located in New York (Porter, Ketels, Habiby, & Zipper, 2008). Attracting a forthcoming successful startup can affect a city tremendously, as the case of Microsoft attests. Although Microsoft is associated with Seattle, the company was founded in 1975 in Albuquerque, New Mexico. Microsoft's subsequent move to Seattle significantly transformed the city. Innovation has the power to reshape the economic fates of entire communities as well as their cultures, urban forms, local amenities, and political attitudes. As Moretti (2012) asserted, human capital is the "best predictor of high salaries both for individuals and for communities.

Local governments increasingly apply the concept of the creative city in their urban regeneration strategies (Mommaas, 2004; Mould, 2014). Areas of concern, such as former warehouses or factories, are turned into centers of new postmodern infrastructure. The buildings in downtown areas such as SoHo in Manhattan once used by squatters, students, or artists are brought back on the real estate market and turned into apartments, lofts, or office spaces (Zukin, 1989). The creative policies are, thereby, used to "recommodify" previously "decommodified areas" (Mommaas, 2004; Zukin, 1989).

Urban leaders are heavily investing in reconverting decaying urban structures, preserving cultural heritage, and investing in the creative industries to attract the creative class (Mould, 2014). The strategy of the creative district is to create a favorable atmosphere for creative individuals to work; to support spin-offs and startups that will attract other creative workers; and to promote trust, socialization, knowledge, inspiration, and incremental innovation in the creative industries characterized by risk and uncertainty (Mommaas, 2004; Mould, 2014). Mould (2014) noted that although those projects are attractive strategies for cities, they do not provide the vibrancy of a creative milieu. Clusters that have emerged from bottom-up are more organic and better able to sustain a creative milieu.

Among all layers of innovation, the creative layer is probably the one in which urban leaders have the slimmest margin for maneuver. Most of the creative layer must grow spontaneously through market forces. Urban leaders can, however, affect market forces by planning the district in a way that enhances its residents' quality of life, as we have seen in the urban planning layer. To generate a healthy creative milieu, urban leaders can also provide low-cost licenses for operating food trucks and street kiosks; low-rent artist workshops; make available no-interest loans or low-rent spaces for independent coffee shops, bars, restaurants, cinemas, bookshops, and stores; build a performance center and/or a museum; loosen regulations for street artists and performers, pop-up events and pop-up bars, restaurants, and stores; promote festivals and congresses; permit graffiti and street art, flying drones, and drinking in the streets; and promote the legalization of "necessary evils" like recreational drugs.

A great source of information for urban leaders who want to learn more about the latest trends in urban amenities attractive to the creative class, entrepreneurs, and knowledge workers is the magazine *Monocle*, which annually ranks cities with the best quality of life globally. In 2015, *Monocle* selected Tokyo, Vienna, Berlin, Melbourne, and Sydney as the five most livable cities in the world. Those cities are highly attractive to the creative class, entrepreneurs, and knowledge workers as a result of their high urban amenities and the vibrant lifestyles they offer.

6

SUCCESS FACTORS

The above-mentioned processes, when employed together, produce innovation. Most of those processes can easily be found in any city; however, they are not as sophisticated nor as integrated in cities as they are in innovation districts. As a result, inefficiencies resulting from a lack of coordination undermine the process of innovation. It is easy to see that the most innovative cities are those where most—if not all—of the processes are present. While we should assume that innovation districts accelerate the process of innovation that does not mean that they will always deliver on this objective. "Build an innovation district and your city will be innovative" is at best a misguided—and at worst a dishonest—statement. Indeed, there are five prerequisites that need to be present in order for innovation districts to accelerate the process of innovation. They are:

(1) An independent organization is created to oversee the development of the innovation district and secure independent funding for an extended period of time—10 to 15 years.

(2) The city has a large population (>400,000 inhabitants) and the necessary critical mass (Gross Metropolitan Product > USD

113

20 billion) to foster knowledge-intensive activities.

(3) The framework is complete and well-integrated, most of the processes are present.

(4) The independent organization aims to constantly upgrade the framework and to strengthen the processes.

(5) The innovation district is resilient to change and open to new concepts and to outsiders.

An innovation district is overseen by an independent organization that has secured funding for the development of the district for a period of 10 to 15 years. The city needs to show a strong commitment to the innovation district in order for it to be successful, and the independent organization should not be too influenced by City Hall or the Mayor's Office. The independent organization needs to be made up of talented individuals who are not technocrats or civil servants, but rather practical people with different backgrounds and experiences, who believe in their city and are committed to making the innovation district a success. Urban leaders must regard an innovation district as an entrepreneurial venture, and need to manage it as such. Innovation districts should not be affected by economic turmoil or local politics. In order to avoid this, it has to obtain secure funding for an extended period of time—at least 10 years—in order to reassure investors, entrepreneurs, companies, and knowledge workers that it is worth it to live, participate, and invest their time and money in the district. In Ohio, a program called the Third Frontier was created to foster entrepreneurship; it began in 2002 and was scheduled to be executed over a period of 10 years. The Third Frontier was successful because entrepreneurs believed in the state's commitment to entrepreneurship.

Innovation districts are successful economic development strategies for cities that have achieved a critical mass in population and wealth. As a rule of thumb, cities aspiring to create innovation districts need to have a metropolitan population of at least 400,000, and a Gross Metropolitan Product of at least USD 20 billion. While there is no maximum limit to the GMP per capita, cities aspiring to build innovation districts should have a GMP per capita of at least USD 5,000. In addition, establishing innovation districts is a successful strategy for Western European and North American cities when their metropolitan populations have reached a minimum of 400,000, while for middle income countries' cities, the metropolitan population should be around 1 to 2 million.

Table 1. Population and GMP are prerequisite elements for innovation districts.

Metropolitan Population	GMP Per Capita (USD)	GMP (Billions USD)
400,000	50,000	20
500,000	40,000	20
700,000	30,000	20
1,000,000	20,000	20
2,000,000	10,000	20
4,000,000	5,000	20

The number of clusters and the size allocated by the city to an innovation district depend upon the metropolitan population and the gross metropolitan product (GMP). A city with a population under 750,000 should always promote diversity-based development with startups, innovative and knowledge companies, and the area allocated should range between 20 and 40 hectares. A city with a metropolitan population of 1,500,000 and a gross metropolitan product of USD 37 billion (GMP per capita of USD 25,000) should allocate between 40 and 60 hectares and pursue the development of one cluster. A city with a metropolitan population of

1,500,000 and a gross metropolitan product of USD 47 billion (GMP per capita of USD 31,000) should allocate between 60 and 90 hectares and pursue the development of two clusters. The rationale behind this distribution is that innovation districts need to be relatively compact and dense while nurturing innovative activities. It follows that a cluster should be adopted as a development strategy when innovation districts have already achieved a resilient critical mass—indeed, developing clusters is a risky endeavor for cities. Although the cluster-based development approach can be successful, it can also be a tremendous failure. As such, relatively small cities should promote only diversity-based development, whereas larger cities should—in addition to diversity-based development—also specialize in handpicked high-growth clusters that are designed in line with their existing strengths.

Table 2. Prerequisites for the number of clusters and the size of an innovation district

Population	GMP (Billions USD)	Cluster	Innovation District (area in hectares)
>400,000	>20	0	20-40
>750,000	>30	1	40-60
>1,250,000	>40	2	60-90
>2,000,000	>55	3	90-120
>3,500,000	>70	4	120-160
>4,000,000	>90	5	160-200

The municipal organization in charge of the transformation of the district into an innovation district needs to have clear key performance indicators for the frameworks and the processes involved. The first objective for the municipal organization is to have a complete framework with sufficient processes to accelerate the innovative capacities of the companies, startups, entrepreneurs, and individuals located or living in the district. The municipal organization has to constantly look to improve and upgrade the different processes. It is important to highlight that the municipal organization will pilot the project for a limited period of time (between 10 and 15 years). Innovation districts work like artificial reefs—instead of nurturing a vibrant marine life, innovation districts nurture innovative companies and startups by providing spaces for innovative and creative individuals to flourish and, in turn, for the district to become a self-sustaining innovation district. Due to the time-constraint, the number and complexity of the processes will determine the success and the sustainability of the innovation district.

Finally, innovation districts are resilient to change and open to new ideas and innovative minds. New ideas and concepts that are deemed positive to innovation will be conceived and added to the processes that I have unveiled. Our sons and grandsons will create new revolutionizing technologies that will stagger us. Innovation districts are resilient to change and rapidly absorb new technological breakthroughs. Innovation districts, like human beings, share the same DNA—they are all agile and adaptable to new paradigms. The capacity to adapt to new technologies and to outsiders will determine the success of the innovation district. Outsiders, weirdos, and passionate individuals are needed to generate new ideas and to constantly challenge the establishment. The next technological wave has to be embraced by innovation districts and not rejected. History shows us that many great cities have fallen because of their inability to reinvent themselves. Innovation districts have to constantly reinvent themselves to become more than a mere district.

Urban leaders should monitor key performance indicators to evaluate the success of their innovation districts. The key performance indicators must include: the number of new startups launched, the number of spinoff companies created, the number of jobs created (skilled and unskilled), the startups' and spinoffs' survival rates, the revenue generated in local taxes, the outside private capital raised by spinoffs and startups, the exit/return on investment for the seed capital companies, the percentage spent on R&D by companies in the innovation district, the population growth (by region, city, and district), the number of associations created, the number of art exhibitions realized, the number of people walking down select streets, etc.

7

CASE STUDIES

The three case studies chosen—Barcelona, Boston, and Singapore—will give readers a practical approach on how cities foster knowledge-based developments with innovation districts. These three case studies are interesting in that three different approaches have been taken to build innovation districts. More interestingly, most of the processes that have been previously discussed are present. Barcelona, a pioneer city in Knowledge-Based Urban Regeneration, is the first city to have designed a large-scale innovation district. Boston has relied on a persuasion exercise with real estate development companies to build its innovation district. Singapore has relied on a strong government leadership to create within a few years a fully operative and integrated innovation ecosystem. The three examples are broad and executed on disparate levels of government intervention—low government intervention in the case of Boston, average government intervention in the case of Barcelona, and high government intervention in the case of Singapore—which reflect how innovation is created at the different institutional levels. The broad scope taken in the three case studies will provide urban leaders with targeted policies for successful innovation district's development strategies.

7.1. 22@ Barcelona

In 2000, the City Council under the leadership of former Mayor Joan Clos, created a municipal company—22 ARROBA BCN S.A.—to pilot 22@ Barcelona, also known as the innovation district, an urban regeneration project in Poblenou, a former industrial district close to Barcelona's city center. 22@ Barcelona is the first innovation district in the world to have been designed by policymakers. In the nineteenth century, Poblenou was the industrial hub of Barcelona. The district was the fifth largest textile producer in the world, then mechanical, chemical, and food-processing industries began flocking into the district (Leon, 2008; López, Romani, Sagarra, & Piqué, 2011). Poblenou was such an important industrial center that it was known as the "Manchester of Catalonia" (Barceló, 2005; López et al., 2011). From 1963 to 1990, more than 1,300 industries left the Poblenou, and Barcelona lost around 250,000 industrial jobs (Duarte & Sabaté, 2013). Transport-related activities ended up occupying the major share of the space, which became gradually abandoned and contributed to the deterioration of the urban environment. In the 1980s, artists began flocking into the district and new activities began to emerge (Oliva, 2003).

The project is based on the Municipal White Paper, *Modificación del PGM para la renovación de las zonas industriales del Poblenou* (in English modification of the General Metropolitan Plan for the transformation of the Poblenou's industrial zones), and aims to transform the old industrial areas of Poblenou into the knowledge and innovation hub of the city. The 22@ Barcelona model is the response of the City Council to the paradigm-shift from mass-production towards the knowledge economy.

22@ Barcelona has three objectives. The first objective is the large-scale urban regeneration of a traditional industrial neighborhood that is located close to downtown Barcelona (Barcelona, 2012; Duarte & Sabaté, 2013; Molas & Sabata, 2011). The strategy to redevelop the industrial area into a 21st-century neighborhood relies on investing in the urban environment with improved transportation (metros, trams, and buses), parks, leisure amenities, broadband telecommunications, renewable energy, sustainable pneumatic garbage collection, and public equipments. The second objective is to attract high-tech industries in five selected clusters: media, information and communication technologies (ICTs), medical technologies, energy, and design (Barcelona, 2012; Duarte & Sabaté, 2013). The third objective is to make Barcelona a leading center of scientific and technological production in the knowledge economy.

The scale of the project and public investment are consequent. Since the 1992 Olympic Games, 22@ Barcelona is the main urban renewal project that the city of Barcelona has undertaken. Indeed, 22@ Barcelona occupies an area of 198.26 hectares (about 115 city blocks) and has a potential occupancy of 4,000,000 m^2, of which 3,200,000 m^2 are intended for productive activities and 800,000 m^2 are intended for other uses, such as housing, spaces for collaboration, and public facilities (Molas & Sabata, 2011). The 22@ Barcelona project aims to create 4,000 new social housing units, regularize 4,614 homes, and build 114,000 m^2 of green spaces and 145,000 m^2 of new public facilities (Battaglia & Tremblay, 2012). The project involves an investment in infrastructure of €180 million funded by Spain, Calonia, the city of Barcelona, and the European Union (Molas & Sabata, 2011). Additionally, the 22@ Barcelona district has the ambition to create 150,000 new jobs in 20 years (Battaglia & Tremblay, 2012).

In ten years, the 22@ district has evolved from an embryonic innovative ecosystem to being a fully integrated innovation district. Today, 22@ Barcelona is a benchmark, and it has achieved recognition from the International Association of Science Parks and the Global Network of Clusters (López et al., 2011). The productive fabric, the number of companies, and the demographic make-up of the innovation district have fundamentally changed over the years. The changing productive typology of the district reflects its transition from industrial to knowledge-intensive. From 2000 to 2011, more than 4,500 new companies have joined the district, of which 31% are knowledge-intensive (22@ Barcelona, 2011). Among the five clusters—ICT, Media, Medical Technologies, Energy, and Design—prioritized by the municipal government, more than half of the companies operating in 22@ Barcelona are part of or related to one of the five clusters (López et al., 2011). Nearly 70% of the companies located in the 22@ Barcelona are SMEs that have less than ten employees (López et al., 2011). Companies located in the 22@ district demonstrate rapid workers' turnover, which is a distinctive trait of spin-offs and startups.

The human capital make-up in the district has, also, widely adjusted to the new knowledge-intensive industries that are located in the district. From 2000 to 2011, 56,000 new professionals began working in the innovation district, of which half of them have a higher education degree (22@ Barcelona, 2011). Critics blame the innovation district to have contributed to the district's gentrification, which is the replacement of a population, mainly artists and unskilled workers, with another seen as more desirable for urban leaders, knowledge workers. From 2000 to 2010, the population of the district has increased by 16,750 inhabitants. In 2010, around 90,000 inhabitants lived in 22@ Barcelona, representing 5.6% of the total population of Barcelona (Molas & Sabata, 2011). As of 2010, 51% of the planned 4,000 social housing have been built or are in construction (Molas & Sabata, 2011).

Leadership

The 22@ Barcelona project emerged from the strategy of Mayor Joan Clos to accelerate the city's transition into the knowledge economy. The 22@ Barcelona district has been modeled from two documents, the "Digital City" and "Barcelona, City of Knowledge," authored by a multidisciplinary team of experts in urban planning, ICT, project management, and economics (Barceló & Oliva, 2002; Trullén 2001). The four pillars of the project are the MPGM22@ (*Modificación del Plan General*

Metropolitano para la renovación de las zonas industriales del Poblenou), the Special Poblenou Infrastructure Plan (PEI), the modification of the Special Plan for Historical/Artistic Architectural Heritage, and the creation of the municipal company 22 ARROBA BCN S.A. (Barceló & Guillot, 2013; López et al., 2011). In this framework, 22 ARROBA BCN S.A. embodies the leadership and long-term commitment of the city for the innovation district; and is thus the foundation of the model and the most important layer in the innovation district's framework.

The main stakeholders are Mayor Joan Clos; urban leaders such as Miquel Barceló and Joan Trullén; the city of Barcelona; Barcelona's urban planning department; various committees (advisory, technical, and heritage); private companies, among which Indra, T-Systems, RBA, Telefonica, Mediapro, and Lavini played a significant role; the residents of the district who voted to approved the project; private landowners; and the real estate development companies (Barceló & Guillot, 2013; López et al., 2011). The different stakeholders that have conceptualized the innovation district share a similar social capital. Indeed, most of the urban leaders involved in the project are from Barcelona and most have graduated from the Universitat Autonoma de Barcelona (UAB).

Branding and communication are important elements of leadership. In 2004, the marketing department of 22@ Barcelona was created and served as a tool to attract real estate development and innovative companies in 22@ Barcelona. The 22@

marketing team mainly targeted two segments: real estate marketing and institutional marketing (Barceló & Guillot, 2013). Real estate marketing aimed to appeal to promoters and real estate development companies. The real estate marketing largely relied on communicating about increased land uses and building permits (Barceló & Guillot, 2013). Institutional marketing aimed to generate awareness of the 22@ district among the public and innovative companies in the five selected clusters (Barceló & Guillot, 2013).

Institutional communications focused on increasing awareness about the district and used national and international branding in order to communicate to companies on the advantages of clusters, and to promote the international recognition and achievement of the innovation district in Spain and overseas (Barceló & Guillot, 2013). The 22@ PLUS initiative was launched in 2008; it was conceived as a value proposition for companies considering to locate in the 22@ district by emphasizing on the value-added elements present in the district, such as technology infrastructure, knowledge infrastructure, business networks, cluster strategies, access to public and private financing, access to talents, access to markets, spaces for collaboration for companies and entrepreneurs, and landing platforms (López et al., 2011).

Urban Planning

Urban planning plays a central role in the 22@ Barcelona model by providing the foundation for the three remaining innovation layers to flourish:

productive, collaborative, and creative. In the innovation district's framework, urban planning is the second layer of innovation to be designed after leadership. Urban planning in the 22@ district is the outcome of three decisive documents: the MPGM22@, the Special Poblenou Infrastructure Plan (PEI), and the Special Plan for Historical/Artistic Architectural Heritage. In 22@ Barcelona, the urban planning framework has four goals: to foster the development of new activities through urban regulations, create diversity, encourage density, and generate a good quality of life. The zoning of the Poblenou district had to adapt to the new productive reality of the innovation district.

All land in the 22@ district belongs to private owners. The MPGM22@ provides incentives for both real estate development companies and private owners to build new spaces by increasing the construction rights to build per square meter of land owned under the condition that the new activities developed are knowledge intensive (Barceló & Guillot, 2013). In addition to contributing to the special infrastructures plan, the developer has to transfer 30% of the built area to the city (Barcelona, 2000). Of that 30%, the city allocates one third to social housing (10% of the total built area), one third to 7@ amenities (10% of the total built area), and one third to green spaces (10% of the total built area) (Barcelona, 2000).

The zoning of the Poblenou district had to adapt to the new productive reality of the innovation district. The important concept is no longer "what" to produce, but "how" to produce it (Trullén, 2011). The

MPGM22@, adopted in 2000, proposes to change the district's zoning from "22a" to "22@," that is, from a strictly industrial zoning to a mixed-use zoning (Barcelona, 2000; Battaglia & Tremblay, 2012; Molas & Sabata, 2011). The "@" refers to the new knowledge-intensive productive activities that were defined according to the OECD (Trullén, 2011). The development of the so-called "@" activities allow private landowners and real estate development companies to build more per square meter of land owned. The urban policies adopted with the MPGM22@ give a strong incentives to promoters and real estate development companies to promote the development of knowledge intensive activities. The MPGM22@ has the ambition to create a mixed-use district by converting industrial activities into residential and productive activities, and thus permitting live-work arrangements (Barceló, 2005). The MPGM22@ aims to increase the complexity, density, and diversity of the district.

Urban complexity, diversity, compactness, and density are achieved through urban policies. The very same policies that Jane Jacobs would eagerly subscribe to. The regulatory structures favor mixed-use activities, mixing different productive activities, the protection of historical buildings (especially former industrial sites), the social housing, and the intensive land uses thanks to relaxed construction rights (Barceló & Guillot, 2013; Barcelona, 2012; Duarte & Sabaté, 2013). In this framework, productive activities coexist with research, training centers with technology transfer offices, residences with businesses, green areas and urban facilities

(Barcelona, 2012). The intended goal is to favor cross-fertilization of ideas and learning among the different actors in the innovation district. Additionally, 22@ Barcelona favors complexity by not defining a precise planning of the district, by protecting historical buildings, and by promoting diversity of activities and socioeconomic backgrounds (Barceló, 2005). It also favors density by incentivizing landowners and real estate development companies to build higher and more-intensively used buildings.

The PEI aims to improve urban infrastructures in 22@ Barcelona. There are plans to upgrade 37 km of streets; build underground galleries; include district heating and cooling; upgrade public transportation; and implement pneumatic waste collection systems, fiber optics, and water management systems (Barcelona Activa, 2012; Espelt-Lleonart, 2012). The PEI aims to promote the district as a showcase of urban best practices in sustainability. In 2010, the level of execution of the PEI was at 39%, 12.7 km of streets had been renovated, and many new infrastructures were in operation (Espelt-Lleonart, 2012). The funding for the PEI stands around €180 million with €9 million coming from the European Union (European Union, 2010). The plan is funded at 60% by landowners, 10% by the city council, and 30% by the city's public service operators (Oliva, 2003). The emphasis on public transportations is to create a new centrality in the city of Barcelona (Trullén, 2011). The transportation plan focuses on bicycles and pedestrians and will provide a new metro line (L9), a tram (Trambesòs), and an AVE high-speed train station linking Barcelona to Paris (Barcelona, 2012; Oliva, 2003). There is a strong emphasis on public transportation and a marked willingness to reduce private transportation by 30% within 10 years (Sabaté & Tironi, 2008). The transportation plan has not only the ambition to reduce the overall carbon footprint of private vehicles but also to make the district an open system to every inhabitant of Barcelona. As an urban regeneration project, 22@ Barcelona reinterprets the function of the old industrial fabric of Poblenou in a contemporary way while preserving the essence of a European city (Barceló, 2005; Charnok & Ribera-Fumaz, 2011). Unlike traditional urban planning, the 22@ district is not preplanned and can organically grow (Barceló, 2005). Urban planners applied New Town planning theories based on mixed-uses, urban density, flexibility, smart infrastructures, compactness, and sustainability. The urban planners aim to foster a high quality of life while promoting diversity, innovation, sustainability, agglomeration economies, complexity, efficiency, and continuity (Barceló, 2005). The approach to not intentionally plan the district, makes it resilient to adapt to emerging trends and technologies.

Productive

The 22@ Barcelona project focuses on knowledge-intensive activities, which are dominated by the "@" activities. The "@" activities were chosen according to the knowledge-intensive activities as classified in the OECD working paper on science, technology, and industry, published in 1991 (Trullén, 2011). The "@" activities are characterized by an intensive use of ICT, a high employment density (workers per surface), the generation of knowledge, the high value added, and their urban features (Barcelona, 2000; Trullén, 2011). Real estate development companies and landowners have the incentive to attract "@" activities to the district thanks to relaxed urban regulations for those activities. As we have seen, the MPGM 22@ permits additional building rights when new buildings dedicate at least 20% of the total built area to "@" activities (Barcelona, 2012).

In 2004, 22@ Barcelona adopted a cluster-based urban development approach and focused on four emerging clusters: media, ICT, medical technologies, and energy (López et al., 2011). The design cluster was added to the list in 2008 (López et al., 2011). The objective of the cluster approach is to reach a competitive position internationally for each cluster. The productive framework developed by the 22@ district positions Barcelona as one of the most forward-thinking cities in innovation and clusters in the world (Barceló, 2005). The 22@ district prioritized the development of five clusters: ICT, media, medical technologies, energy, and design. Those clusters were selected following a top-down strategy of governance on the basis of potential growth and prior capabilities (Battaglia & Tremblay, 2012). Companies belonging to one of the five clusters are advised to locate in well-defined areas within the innovation district. The clusters were selected to locate in the district to cross-fertilize each other and create additional intellectual synergy. Of the five clusters of 22@ Barcelona, the media cluster is the most advanced (Barceló & Guillot, 2013). The media cluster intends to have 115,000 m^2 for businesses and 60,000 m^2 for facilities that will include public institutions, private companies, the Pompeu Fabra communication campus, the Barcelona Media Park, the Barcelona Media Innovation Center, private residences, incubators, and Spaces for Collaboration (SFC) such as the MediaTic Building (Barceló & Guillot, 2013). The 22@ district has also created a free-trade zone for mobile technology companies as well as incentive packages (tax breaks and rent subsidies) to attract innovative companies into the media and ICT clusters (Mobile World Capital, 2012). Each year the Mobile World Congress is held in Barcelona in order to showcase and promote the latest mobile technologies.

The 22@ district aims to attract entrepreneurs and foster entrepreneurship. Barcelona has launched 22@ Emprendedores (*entrepreneurs* in English) to create the suitable conditions for 22@ Barcelona to become a magnet for entrepreneurs (Barceló, 2005). The 22@ district launched many projects and created many incentives to foster entrepreneurship, such as Barcelona Activa, which is the largest public business incubator in Europe; the MediaTic building, a space in which incubators, consultants, seed accelerators, and entrepreneurs are co-working together; 22@ landing platforms in which startups can rent offices on a weekly or monthly basis; and residences for entrepreneurs (22@ Barcelona, n.d.).

Collaborative

The ultimate role of the 22@ district is to facilitate innovation. Collaboration between many different actors is seen as central in the process of innovation. Innovation is increasingly seen not only as a critical component of national and regional economic development, but possibly as the most important component for wealth creation (Fisher, 2006). Innovation is closely associated with knowledge, innovation, and in a narrower sense, it may be defined as the application of knowledge (Fisher, 2006).

The 22@ Barcelona project has adopted the European Commission's definition of innovation. The European Commission (1996) defines innovation as "the commercially successful exploitation of new technologies, ideas or methods through the introduction of new products or processes, or through the improvement of existing ones; innovation is a result of an interactive learning process that involves often several actors from inside and outside the companies" (p. 54).

The 22@ Barcelona model is based on the triple helix model of innovation, in which companies, universities, and public institutions work together to achieve breakthrough innovation (Etzkowitz & Piqué, 2011). Each cluster is represented by an ecosystem of public institutions and a university. The media cluster, with the creation of the Barcelona Media Park for instance, is the result of a collaboration between a public university (Universidad Pompeu Fabra), a leading private company in the Catalonian audiovisual sector (Mediapro), several entities from the Barcelona City Hall (Department for Culture, Local Development Agency, 22@ Barcelona), and the regional government (Center for Corporate Innovation and Development) (Barceló, 2005). In this new paradigm, companies from the different clusters, public institutions, and universities cooperate to innovate, create spinoffs, and generate a productive labor force.

At the center of the collaborative layer in 22@ Barcelona are the Spaces For Collaboration (SFC), known in Barcelona as "7@ amenities," which are created from the compulsory land transfers as regulated by the MPGM 22@. Indeed, 10% of the converted spaces are used to sustain the 7@ amenities to house university centers for scientific and technological innovation, such as IESE, ESADE, EADA, UB, UAB, UPC, UPF, URL, UIC, UOC, and IAAC; R&D laboratories; landing platforms for entrepreneurs; and training centers (Barceló, 2005). The 7@ amenities are defined as centers of diffusion of new technologies (Barcelona, 2000). The 7@ amenities' mission is twofold. First, they aim to prevent a digital divide by diffusing new technologies to the population (Oliva, 2003). The "7@" are designed for the population at large. Second, they aim to be spaces to foster innovation through collaboration. The "7@" are spaces for collaboration designed to favor proximity and the spread of tacit knowledge. One of the 7@ flagship initiatives is the MediaTic building. The building, inaugurated in September 2010, covers an area of 14,000 m^2 and serves as a communication hub and a meeting point for businesses, students, entrepreneurs, R&D centers, and institutions in the field of ICT (Barcelona Activa, 2012). The building is divided in three parts: two floors are for common uses; four floors are reserved for entrepreneurs, venture capital firms, seed accelerators, and the landing platforms; and three floors are reserved for private companies and public institutions (Barcelona Activa, 2012). The building hosts the following institutions: Barcelona digital; technological centers; the Internet Interdisciplinary Institute (IN3); the elearn center; the cibernarium (a digital training center for professionals and companies); landing platforms for entrepreneurs; and the open university of Catalunia (Barcelona Activa, 2012). The MediaTic building is the flagship "7@" that not only functions as a working space but also as public space spurring collaboration and experimentation between many diverse actors.

The 22@ Barcelona model is designed on two key assets: tacit knowledge and proximity. It implies that in a certain environment, like 22@, knowledge spreads faster and collaboration is easier. The territoriality of innovation is contained to respond to the new knowledge economy paradigm, where the production of innovation is increasingly localized. The initiatives taken by 22@ Barcelona to foster tacit knowledge and proximity are 22@ Synergys, 22@ Breakfast, 22@ Urban Labs, 22@ Tecnologico, the Smart City Campus, and 22@ Networking. In the above-mentioned initiatives, the different actors and stakeholders meet and exchange new ideas and new way of doing things.

The 22@ Synergys initiative aims to promote collaboration between the research community and the industries at the European and global level by providing open platforms for conferences, debates, and collaboration (Granados, 2011). The 22@ Tecnologico innovation comprises centers for dissemination of new technologies and aims to ease the transfer of innovation to the market (Barceló, 2005). The 22@ Urban Labs spaces are for experimentation and for testing new products and urban services (Barcelona, 2012). The 22@ Urban Labs has given municipal governments a new role in managing platforms and ecosystems in which companies and citizens test prototypes in an urban context (Almirall & Chesbrough, 2011; Granados, 2011; Majó, 2011). In this context, the urban labs serve as a medium for open innovation (Almirall & Chesbrough, 2011; Majó, 2011). The Smart City Campus, which was founded in 2011, is a new space for urban innovation that brings together companies; institutions; universities; and research centers in ICT, innovation ecosystems, and urban planning (Barcelona, 2012). Those initiatives aim to spread new ideas, cross-fertilize existing ones, and improve the district's overall efficiency through smart technologies.

Creative

The creative layer complements the four previous layers of innovation. For creative urban thinkers such as Richard Florida and Charles Landry, creative individuals are central to the process of innovation. The final layer of the 22@ Barcelona model becomes functional through the regulatory frameworks imposed on the urban, the productive, and the collaborative plans. Miquel Barceló, director of 22@ Barcelona, has modeled the 22@ Barcelona project around the ideas of Richard Florida and the concept of the creative class (Barceló, 2005). The urban planning layer aims to recreate an attractive atmosphere for the creative class, like the Chelsea neighborhood in New York City, and other creative districts and cities that have been visited during the "Digital City" project (Ballester, 2013; Barceló & Guillot, 2013; Barcelona, 2000). For Barceló (2005), cities not only have to attract companies but also talented knowledge workers and creative individuals.

The 22@ district creates an atmosphere in which old industrial buildings coexist with modern ones. In 2006, the city of Barcelona modified its Catalogue of Heritage Sites to include 114 new historical buildings in the 22@ district (Barcelona, 2012). The historical buildings are being rehabilitated into @ activities with Can Culleres Spoon factory; 7@ amenities with Ca l'Aranyó, Can Jaumandreu, Can Ricart, and Can Framis, where Vila Casas Foundation is located; and lofts with Passage of Sucre and Can Gili Nou (Barcelona, 2012). The preservation and conversion of the historical buildings aim to foster a sense of identity and community, as well as reinforcing the quality of the district (Florida, 2002). The conservation of the industrial sites create a sense of authenticity that is prized by the creative class.

The 22@ innovation district is modeled in accordance with the specific lifestyle preferences of the creative class and young professionals, such as the richness of cultural activities, bike lanes, walkable streets, a good nightlife, loft living, an abundance of third places, parks, restaurants, diversity, and the rehabilitation of historic buildings. In this framework, the urban planning layer aims to capture and attract the creative class to live, work, and play in the district. The 22@ district is planned in a way to improve and upgrade urban services, such as renewable energy, public transportation, centralized air conditioning, broadband, fiber optics, use of groundwater, and network pneumatic waste collection (Barcelona, 2012). The old factories, such as the emblematic Can Ricart or Can Framis factory, are converted into lofts, museums, and public spaces (Sabaté & Tironi, 2008). Barcelona is today an attractive city for the creative class. Indeed, 55% of the international community (from the European Union, United States, and Canada) over the age of 18 has a higher education degree, more than double that of the local population (Leon, 2007).

Barceló and Guillot (2013) described the strategies involved in activating the creative city in the 22@ district. The techno-creative 22@ district is defined by its flexibility, multidimensionality, and multilayered innovation processes, which facilitate the rise of creative industries. The elements accelerating the transition toward the creative city include connectivity, identity, talents, culture, innovative culture, and a sense of community (Barceló & Guillot, 2013). The 22@ district is now adopting specific strategies to establish a creative district by fostering an international culture, creating networks with the IN22@, opening museums (e.g.,

Museum of Design of Barcelona, and Vila Casas Foundation in Can Framis), and promoting cultural events (e.g., exhibitions, concerts, festivals); reinforcing a strong district identity and sense of community with district associations such as 22@ Poblenou; promoting a good quality of life and a family friendly environment with green areas (e.g., Barcelona Central Park) and sport activities (e.g., Can Ricart, shared bicycles); creating shared spaces for entrepreneurs, professionals, and students (e.g., landing platforms, Melon district residences); attracting and building talents with the 22@ Creatalent and 22@ Staying in Company; and promoting an innovative and digital culture with educational programs (Barceló, 2005; Barceló & Guillot, 2013; Granados, 2011; Pareja-Eastway, 2011). The creative layer emphasizes on creating a sense of community and belongings, which then translate into trust, cooperation, and collaboration.

Figure 3. Overview of 22@ Barcelona Framework

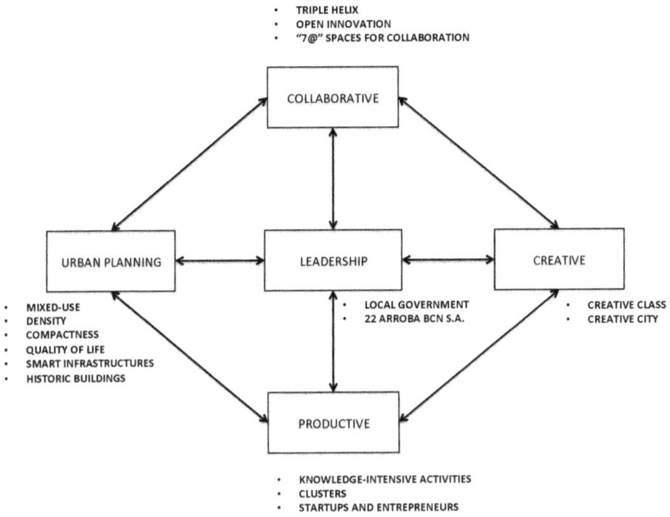

7.2. Boston's Innovation District

In 2010, former Mayor Thomas Menino inaugurated Boston's Innovation District. Boston's Innovation District is located in the South Boston waterfront next to Boston's Central Business District. The purpose of the innovation district is to transform 1,000 acres (405 hectares) of South Boston Waterfront property into an urban environment that fosters innovation, collaboration, and entrepreneurship (Sharma, 2012). Since 2010, the innovation district has brought 4,000 new jobs and more than 200 new companies to the City of Boston (Boston Redevelopment Authority, 2014a). The area includes four districts: Fort Point, Fan Pier, the Seaport World Trade Center, and Boston Marine

Industrial Park (BMIP). Among those four districts that compose Boston's Innovation District, the Fort Point neighborhood and Boston's Marine Industrial Park had already profoundly transformed themselves. The Fort Point neighborhood was dubbed the Cyber District during the dot-com bubble and was a magnet for Internet start-ups. The Boston Marine Industrial Park is the city's initiative to promote maritime industries and the ocean trade. Moreover, megaprojects, such as the Big Dig and the Institute of Contemporary Arts (ICA), that were realized in the past decade, contributed to make the South Waterfront an attractive area to redevelop.

Boston's Innovation District includes the Boston Marine Industrial Park (BMIP), which is owned by the city's Economic Development and Industrial Corporation (EDIC). The area was formerly an Army and Naval base that was abandoned until the property was granted to the EDIC (BRA, 2014b). The area was first identified as a prime location for consolidating, preserving, and growing Boston's ocean trade, maritime industries, and industrial uses before being incorporated into Boston's innovation district. The Marine Industrial Park is home to the Innovation and Design Building and Mass Challenge, the world's largest start-up accelerator.

In the 19th century, the Fort Point Channel area was the center of Boston's wool and shoe industry (Barcelona, 2000; Kotkin & DeVol, 2001). With the decline of the textile and leather industries in the beginning of the 20th century, the large warehouses, department stores, and manufacturing plants were gradually abandoned. In the 1970s and 1980s, the area began to attract artists seeking inexpensive, centrally located spaces (Kotkin & DeVol, 2001). In the early 1990s, the area began to attract specialized media, advertising, and Internet software firms. At this time, the Fort Point Channel area became known as the Cyber District. By the end of 1998, the Cyber District included 350 high-tech companies (primarily Internet start-ups) that employed approximately 3,500 people (Barcelona, 2000). The Cyber District emerged from a bottom-up process. Indeed, the so-called Cyber District grew spontaneously through market forces without any intervention from the city of Boston. The district was attractive for startups due to the below-average real estate prices that allowed the companies to rehabilitate old brick warehouses and abandoned factories (Kotkin & DeVol, 2001).

As for the Poblenou district in Barcelona, South Boston's waterfront is adjacent to the city's downtown and was a relatively under- and undeveloped area with abandoned warehouses, brownfield lands, and empty parking lots. In the past decades, the Marine Industrial Park section and the Fort Point neighborhood of what would become the innovation district began to attract biotech, clean tech, and start-up companies. As a result, the potential to purposefully grow a cluster of innovative companies made the South Boston Waterfront location a natural fit for the development of Boston's Innovation District. Mayor Thomas Menino developed the innovation district to pursue an agenda centered on shared innovation. The project has a surface of 1,000 acres, roughly 404.67 hectares, and officially debuted in 2010. The innovation district has the objective to transform the South Boston Waterfront into a 24-hour neighborhood that fosters innovation, collaboration, and entrepreneurship (BRA, 2013a).

The ambition of Boston's Innovation District is threefold, it aims: to transform an underused area of the city into an "agile" neighborhood, to promote and foster entrepreneurship, and to maintain Boston's competitiveness. The strategy and goals of Boston's Innovation District were noticeably captured in Mayor Menino's speech when he announced the Seaport Square project in 2010, saying, "to be bold, creative, and keep our economy growing. Together, we are creating a unique, diverse, and entrepreneurial neighborhood that will help Boston attract and retain new industries and the city's young, talented workforce" (BRA, 2010a).

First, Boston's Innovation District seeks to transform the South Boston Waterfront into Boston's first 21st-century neighborhood. The innovation district is intended to be built continually over decades, and it will include sustainable transportation systems, sustainable designs, and public amenities. The "agile" neighborhood strategy intends to promote continuous innovation and foster experimentation at the urban and architectural level (Mitch Weiss, personal communication, November 17, 2014).

Second, Boston's Innovation District aims to promote and foster entrepreneurship. Babson College has recently relocated its highly ranked program in entrepreneurship to the district. This facility, which opened in 2011, provides an opportunity for entrepreneurial students interested in MBA courses to take them in a location convenient to where the students live and work (Babson, n.d.). Moreover, Boston is home to the highest concentration of young adults (20–34 years old) among the 25 largest cities in the United States (BRA, 2013b). Indeed, 35% of Boston's population is young adults; however, many of those young adults who are enrolled in one of the city's 35 colleges, universities, and community colleges, leave the city as soon as they earn their degrees (BRA, 2013c).

As shown by Wadhwa, Freeman, and Rissing (2010), the proportion of tech-founders who establish a start-up in the same state in which they earned their academic degrees is below average in Massachusetts with only 29% of graduates, compared with 69% in California. The focus on entrepreneurship has, as a result, a twofold ambition: to attract and retain young college graduates in the city and to foster the creation of innovative start-ups.

Third, Boston's Innovation District aims to maintain the city's competitiveness. The relative decline of Route 128 against new emerging knowledge hubs such as Austin, TX, downtown Palo Alto, downtown San Francisco, Tech City in London, and the Silicon Alley in New York City for instance, signal that businesses are moving back to the cities' downtowns (Florida, 2012). New York City, with the Silicon Alley, is now the second tech hub in the United States after the Silicon Valley (Bowles & Gilles, 2012). The success of the Silicon Alley is attributed to its urban features that attract tech entrepreneurs and knowledge workers. Innovative start-ups prefer to be located in cities rather than in suburban office parks like Route 128, and the city of Boston with the Boston's innovation district aims to readjust itself to this new reality. Indeed, the United States' seed and early stage venture-capital investment dollars compiled by the National Venture Capital Association (NVCA) and PricewaterhouseCoopers (PwC) in 2013 show that the State of Massachusetts (mostly Route 128 and Cambridge) with $ 3.1 billion is being tailgated by the State of New York (mostly the Silicon Alley) with $ 2.9 billion and to a lesser extent by the State of Texas (mostly Austin) with $ 1.3 billion.

Boston's Innovation District is modeled on 22@ Barcelona. Although Boston has not rigorously copied the 22@ Barcelona model, it has incorporated some of the urban features that characterized the 22@ district (Mitch Weiss, personal communication, November 17, 2014). As a result, it incorporates the five layers of innovation that are involved in the 22@ Barcelona's model, which are: leadership, urban planning, productive, collaborative, and creative.

Leadership

The main stakeholders that have participated in the design of Boston's Innovation District are: the former mayor of Boston Thomas Menino; the mayor's office; the City of Boston; the Boston Redevelopment Authority (BRA); and the real estate developers. The Boston Redevelopment Authority is the urban planning and economic development agency for the City of Boston that has been aligning the mayor's vision with that of the real estate development companies. The BRA and the city of Boston have taken part in ongoing negotiation with real estate development companies to instill innovation features in their plans. Indeed, the real estate developers wanted to build traditional housing and commercial projects, like luxury condominiums and shopping malls; Mayor Thomas Menino, the City of Boston, and Boston Redevelopment Authority had to persuade real estate development companies to build untraditional projects (Mitch Weiss, personal communication, November 17, 2014). Among the real estate development companies that are participating in developing the South Boston Waterfront, the most notable ones are Cresset Development, with the $60 million three-building complex named Liberty Wharf (Ross, 2010); Gale International, Morgan Stanley, and W/S Development Associates with the 23-acre, 6.3 million square foot, $3 billion master plan project Seaport Square (BRA, 2010a); and the Drew Company, with the 350,000 square feet mixed-use Waterside Place (BRA, 2014c). Gale International and Morgan Stanley are also developing the Songdo International Business District in South Korea, a $35 billion Smart city project and one of the largest real estate development projects in history (Gale International, n.d.).

The city is not using a local economic development strategy with public funding and incentives to drive businesses into the area; instead, the city is using public relations to encourage entrepreneurs and start-ups to relocate to the district. The BRA has been negotiating with real estate development companies to instill some innovative components into their plans. The approach adopted to create Boston's Innovation District is thus a top-down negotiation between Boston Redevelopment Authority and real estate development companies.

Urban Planning

As for 22@ Barcelona, urban planning is central in Boston's Innovation District. It is through urban planning that the innovation district is being created. Because the majority of the land is privately held, the financial burden of this initiative will not fall on the City of Boston, but the real estate development companies. The strategy to spur innovation in the newly created innovation district has been for the city of Boston to work with real estate developers to instill innovative features into their plans.

The Seaport Square's project embodies Mayor Menino's vision; it is the cornerstone of the innovation district's ambitious strategy (BRA, 2010b). Seaport Square is being developed by Gale International, Morgan Stanley, and W/S Development Associates and will be a 23-acre (approximately 9.3 hectares), 6.5 million square feet (approximately 600,000 square meters), $ 3 billion master plan project that will be composed of 2.75 million square feet (approximately 250,000 square meters) of residential, 1.25 million square feet (approximately 115,000 square meters) of retail, 1.4 million square feet (approximately 130,000 square meters) of office and research, 500,000 square feet (approximately 45,000 square meters) of hotel, and 600,000 square feet (approximately 55,000 square meters) of educational, civic, and cultural uses (BRA, 2010a; BRA, 2010b). It will be the largest development project in Boston's history (BRA, 2010b). The real estate development companies have had to consult with the BRA over a yearlong period to develop the Seaport Square master plan in order to incorporate elements in the plan that focus on the public realm, the program of uses, infrastructures, sustainability, and sensitivity to context (BRA, 2010b). The project is intended to be gradually built over 7 to 10 years, with state-of-the-art sustainability and public amenities designed to enhance the neighborhood (BRA, 2010b). It will be Boston's first 21st-century neighborhood and will combine the essence of historic Boston "with 21st century concepts of livability, sustainability, and global competitiveness" (BRA, 2010b). Seaport Square aims to become a 24-hour, mixed-use neighborhood not only horizontally layered but also vertically layered with young and old, rich and poor, businessmen and students, hotel workers and scientists, visitors and Bostonians (BRA, 2010b). The Seaport Square is a mixed-use, diverse, and sustainable district. Those characteristics promote serendipity encounters among diverse people and will foster collaboration, and hence accelerate the process of innovation.

The BRA is negotiating with real estate development companies in order for their projects to incorporate specific innovative amenities. In the Seaport Square project for instance, the project will include at least 20% of "Innovation Uses" of built floor area of the total gross floor area of the project's nonresidential uses (BRA, 2010b). The Innovation

Uses include: laboratories, small business incubators, public event spaces for exhibitions, rooftop gardens, the District Hall, retail businesses, hotels, innovation transportation and energy, and public, common, or shared spaces within innovation/workforce housing (BRA, 2010b). The new civic, cultural, and community contributions include a performing arts center, flexible gallery spaces, educational facilities, a public library, and a Catholic chapel (BRA, 2010b). The project will also improve the existing infrastructures and create new infrastructures (BRA, 2010b). The project's contributions include new streets and sidewalks, new pedestrian connections, the Northern Avenue Bridge, open spaces and landscape improvements, and a public art trail (BRA, 2010b). The innovative spaces aim to attract and stimulate people with a certain entrepreneurial spirit.

Among the new Innovation Uses, the District Hall, the innovation space, and the innovation housing are pioneer urban planning practices. The District Hall, which opened in 2013, is a 12,000-square-foot (approximately 1,100 square meters) center for innovation and is leased by the real estate development companies to the BRA and the city of Boston for $1 per year for a minimum period of 5 years with renewable rights for an additional period of 5 years (BRA, 2010b). Additionally, the Seaport Square developers will lease at least 12,000 square feet (approximately 1,100 square meters) of innovation space to a tenant or tenants for uses consistent with the mayor's Innovation District initiatives for a period of 15 years (BRA, 2010b). The innovation housing units aim to attract specific residents and to meet the needs of a diverse workforce, namely knowledge workers and artists (commonly referred as the creative class). The innovation housings are described by the BRA as cohousing or live-work spaces, which may include smaller unit sizes, flexible unit layouts, combined living and working spaces, and a common space shared by residents occupying different units (BRA, 2010b). The innovation housing units are nearby urban amenities such as co-working spaces, incubator space, restaurants and sidewalk cafes (BRA, 2010b). The amenities serve as third places or more accurately as an extension of the innovation housings due to the relative alienation of living alone in micro-apartments. The project will also include approximately 5,000 square feet of cultural and/or educational space (BRA, 2010b). The cultural and educational spaces promote continuous learning, creativity, and self-expression.

In the City of Boston, specific policies regulate housing for residential projects. Real estate development companies have the duty to build a percentage of affordable and workforce housing units. Concerning affordable housing, the mayor's executive order dated May 16, 2006 established that any residential project seeking zoning relief must set aside at least 15% of the number of market rate units as affordable housing to middle-income households (BRA, 2010b). Concerning workforce housing, it is intended for people whose income is too high to qualify for formally restricted affordable housing units but who are often priced out of the housing market. Workforce housing and affordable housing aim to instill diversity (BRA, 2010b). In the Seaport Square project, 325 units of affordable housing units and 325 workforce housing units will be handed over (BRA, 2010b). Residential policies aim to favor diversity and to limit the negative effects of gentrification in the innovation district.

The South Boston Waterfront Sustainable Transportation Plan (2014) is being developed both as a strategic plan and as an action plan to build the innovation district as a 21st century neighborhood. It seeks to analyze and monitor trends in order to offer the most efficient transportation to the district and provide a blueprint for the transportation system improvement over a 20-year-planning horizon. It defines strategies to address existing transportation and mobility issues in the neighborhood; capacity constraints; transit, pedestrian, and bicycle needs; and operational enhancements. Creating a multimodal transportation system is central. The multimodal transportation system includes: public bicycle sharing system with the Hubway; car-rental service with Zipcar; additional bus routes; and the MBTA Silver Line. The multimodal transportation system contributes to enhance the attractiveness and accessibility of the innovation district to Boston's residents.

Productive

Boston's Innovation District aims to provide amenities to attract innovative start-ups and entrepreneurs. Indeed, 25% of the new companies that have located in Boston's Innovation District since 2010 are of small scale, with 10 or fewer employees (www.innovationdistrict.org). Chatterji, Glaeser, and Kerr (2013) explained the approach taken by Boston's Innovation District toward entrepreneurship:

> "Cluster policies for entrepreneurship and innovation occupy a very distinct place in this scheme. They are narrowly place-specific, favoring a very specific locale, such as Boston's Innovation District. This geographic concentration is justified both as a tool for generating positive externalities and as a means of getting the most out of scarce infrastructure dollars. They are also oriented towards either specific industrial sectors (life science, computers) or more generally towards start-ups. They are not usually firm-specific, largely because start-ups are too small to address on a firm-by-firm basis, but also because the proponents of these policies often share economists' skepticism about the ability to pick winning firms, even though they believe in the ability to pick winning sectors." (p.6)

The innovation district has adopted a diversity strategy that does not target any specific industry or cluster. The local government sees the diversity strategy as a less costly and risky endeavor than a cluster strategy. While in the event of the cluster's slowdown, the innovation district would have faced a severe crisis; a diversity strategy makes the innovation more resilient to economic crises and to Kondratieff cycles. The City of Boston and the Boston Redevelopment Authority, like New York

City under mayor Bloomberg (Porter et al., 2008), aim to attract start-ups in the district by providing appropriate spaces (co-working spaces and collaborative spaces), infrastructures (public and private infrastructures), and highly skilled workforce (the creative class). In Boston's innovation district, the talented professionals and knowledge workers will be attracted to the district because of the high quality of life (urban amenities) and the convenient housing options (innovation housing units). The ultimate objective of this competitive strategy is that innovative companies and start-ups will choose to freely locate in the district in order gain a sustained competitive advantage from being in the innovation district rather than because they were offered more fiscal and economic incentives to locate here than elsewhere.

One of those initiatives to attract start-ups in the district is the Innovation and Design Building that was built in the early 1900s as storage space for the South Boston Army Base. The real estate developer, Jamestown, is converting/reclassifying 206,388 square feet (approximately 20,000 square meters) of interior space from its current industrial or vacant use to commercial use (Keith, 2014). The building is home to MassChallenge, the world's largest start-up seed accelerator. The Innovation and Design Building seeks to mimic the San Francisco Chronicle Building's success in attracting large Internet start-ups such as Yahoo Inc. (Keith, 2014).

Collaborative

The District Hall, opened in 2013, is the showcase of the innovative strategy declared by the Boston Redevelopment Authority and former Mayor Thomas Menino's office. The District Hall proclaims itself as "the world's first free-standing public innovation center and a dedicated civic space where the innovation community can gather and exchange ideas" (www.districthallboston.org). The District Hall is operated by BRA and the Cambridge Innovation Center, a company providing spaces for start-ups in Kendall Square in Cambridge. The District Hall includes a restaurant, a café, co-working spaces, and event centers for networking events, conferences, or panels of experts.

Innovation Housing and Innovation Uses are part of the BRA's objective to promote live, work, and play spaces that will in turn foster collaboration, and the spread of tacit knowledge through proximity. The principle is to promote collaboration via the creation of shared spaces. The close proximity of start-ups and entrepreneurs in the district will lead to the sharing of knowledge and technologies, thus accelerating the process of innovation.

Vertex Pharmaceuticals, the developer of the hepatitis C vaccine, opened a 1.1 million-square-foot office and lab space in 2014 in the Innovation District (BRA, 2014d). It signals to start-ups and entrepreneurs the potential for spin-offs and collaboration. The presence of large firms in the district signals to smaller firms that they will be able to connect with potential investors, partners, and suppliers and thus creates a cumulative causation, attracting more start-ups in the innovation district. The presence of large innovative firms confers to newly created startups an innovative legitimacy.

The triple helix model of innovation is not applied in Boston's Innovation District because the local government does not act "as a public entrepreneur and venture capitalist in addition to its traditional regulatory role in setting the rules of the game" (Etzkowitz, 2003). The City of Boston and Boston Redevelopment Authority, however, take a more laissez-faire approach that follows the traditional university-industry double helices model of innovation that is commonly applied in the United States. Universities in the United States are entrepreneurial in that the knowledge they create is put to productive uses. The goal in Boston's Innovation District is to create an innovation ecosystem similar to the one found in Cambridge (Massachusetts), where spinoffs are the product of academic research at the Massachusetts Institute of Technology (MIT) or Harvard University among many other universities, and/or private companies.

Creative

Boston's Innovation District clearly asserts its willingness to attract the creative class as defined by Richard Florida. The millennials are the prime targets of the real estate developments and are parts of the city's strategy to retain its young, educated workforce. In 2004, the City of Boston launched, under Mayor Menino's leadership, ONEin3 to "connect Boston's young adult population with resources related to housing, professional development, financial health, entrepreneurship, and civic engagement" (www.onein3boston.com). Indeed, 35% of Boston's population comprises young adults, of which 48% hold a bachelor's degree or higher (www.onein3boston.com). Young adults add $1 billion annually to Boston's gross product and supports 22,241 additional jobs in the city's economy (www.onein3boston.com). It is for those reasons that Boston's Innovation District focuses on attracting and retaining young adults, who additionally represent a big chunk of Boston's creative class.

To attract the creative class into Boston's Innovation District, the following strategies were adopted.

First, BRA appealed to real estate developers to build "Innovation Housing Units," also known as micro apartments, which combine living, shared, and working spaces. The Innovation Housings are exclusively designed to appeal to young singletons. Mayor Menino had to alter city regulations, from a minimum apartment's dimensions of 450 square feet (roughly 42 square meters) down to 300 square feet (roughly 28 square meters) in order to allow for the construction of the innovation housing units (Acitelli, 2011). Rents are estimated to be between $1,500 and $2,000 per month for 400 square feet and 500 square feet innovation housing units (boston.com, n.d.). The Distillery Project on 516-524 East Second Street is one example of such real estate developments to attract the creative class. The project contains 65 residential units, including a mix of artist live/work, loft-style, and conventional units, 147 parking spaces, an art gallery, a greenhouse, and small-scale retail spaces. To make the place more authentic, the existing distillery building was preserved (boston.com, n.d.).

Second, the Innovation Uses that are required to be built in certain real estate development projects like Seaport Square directly appeal to the creative class. Indeed, the Innovation Uses include urban amenities to transform the district into a 24-hour neighborhood with the right mix of eclectic nightlife and working spaces. The innovation uses include: restaurants, bars, coffee places that will foster lively streets and contribute to make the innovation district attractive neighborhood to work, live, and play.

Third, the Institute of Contemporary Art (ICA), which opened in 2006, is located in the innovation district. The innovation district aims to provide the basic elements of a creative city through public amenities such as the sculptures garden, renovated lofts, Third Places, and parks. Moreover, the BRA provides funds for diverse social projects in the innovation district. Among those projects, the BRA has fund $100,000 to the Fort Point Arts Community, Inc. (FPAC), a non-profit arts organization that promotes local artists, fosters local art initiatives, and seeks to preserve artists housing (BRA, 2013d).

The industries that have located in the district are from creative fields. Among the 5,000 new jobs and 200 new companies that have located themselves in Boston's Innovation District, technology companies have contributed to 30% of new job growth; 21% of new jobs are in creative industries such as design and advertising, 16% of new jobs are in the greentech and life science sectors, and 11% of the jobs are in the education and nonprofit sector (www.innovationdistrict.org). The numerous co-working spaces, shared spaces along with the start-up accelerator such as Mass Challenge, have played an important role in attracting new residents in the innovation district. Indeed, 40% of the new companies established in the innovation district are located in co-working spaces and start-up incubators (www.innovationdistrict.org).

Figure 4. Overview of Boston's Innovation District Framework.

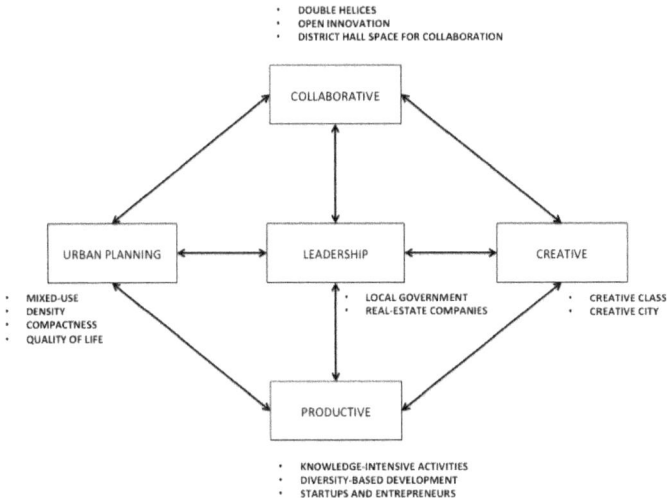

7.3. one-north Singapore

Singapore is a city-state that gained independence from Malaysia in 1965. From 1965 to

2015, the population has grown from 1.6 million to 5 million, while its economy has grown a hundredfold. Singapore moved quickly through major stages of economic development from labor-intensive in the 1960s and 1970s, to skill intensive in the 1980s, to technology-intensive in the 1990s, to knowledge-intensive in the 2010s. GDP per capita has grown from US$512 in 1965 to US$55,000 in 2014. In 1997, Singapore was hit hard by the Asian financial crisis. Singapore's leaders understood that the small city-state had to transform itself into a knowledge hub in order to become resilient to future economic crises. One-north was at the center of the government strategy to Singapore's transition toward the knowledge economy. One-north was launched in 2001, comprises a total area of 182 hectares, and is a US$8.6 billion project. One-north has the characteristics of an innovation district in that the area combines leadership, urban planning, productive, collaborative, and creative layers of innovation.

Leadership

In 2000, the JTC Corporation, a statutory board under the Ministry of Trade and Industry (MTI), was appointed to lead the development of one-north. The Agency for Science Technology and Research (A*Star), the Economic Development Board (EDB), the Standards, Productivity and Innovation Board (SPRING), the Urban Redevelopment Authority, the Singapore Land Authority are the main agencies that are participating in the development of one-north. One-north was launched under Deputy Prime Minister Dr Tony Tan Keng Yam who stated during the opening speech that one-north had three objectives: (1) to be a magnet for talent; (2) to integrate, synergize, and encourage cross-disciplinary research; (3) to bridge the private sector and public sector research work by creating an environment that fosters exchange of ideas and close collaboration.

Urban Planning

One-north is strategically located next to the National University of Singapore, the National University Hospital, Singapore Science Park, and the Ministry of Education. The master plan was designed by the starchitect Zaha Hadid. One-north is a compact, dense, walkable, and mixed-use district. The comprehensive mixed-use approach is promoted as a live-work-play-learn community. Indeed, one-north includes offices, laboratories, universities, schools, residences, condominiums, a shopping mall, restaurants, bars, and nightlife. The different clusters are interconnected with a central green corridor. One-north is easily accessible with three metro stations located within the district. On Portsdown Road, black-and-white houses that were formerly living quarters for British military personnel were preserved as heritage site.

Productive

One-north has three clusters, Biopolis, Fusionopolis, and Mediapolis. The three clusters are dedicated to biomedical, ICTs, and media activities respectively. In Biopolis for instance, the buildings have ancient Greek names indicating the kinds of activities supported. Genome houses the Genome Institute of Singapore; Nanos has the Institute of

Bioengineering and Nanotechnology; and Proteos houses the Institute of Molecular and Cell Biology. Biopolis aims to become the biomedical hub of Asia. There is a strong focus on entrepreneurship in one-north with the Launchpad, a space strictly dedicated to startups. The Launchpad will house around 500 startups and 35 incubators as well as restaurants. The government has also adopted a liberal immigration policy to attract entrepreneurs from overseas. Singapore with its heavy handed government lack an entrepreneurship culture. One-north has the objective to unleash the entrepreneurial spirit of Singaporeans.

Collaborative

One-north has adopted the Triple-Helix model of innovation, and has built spaces for collaboration within the district. In Biopolis for instance, research institutes, universities, and private companies collaborate to foster innovations. The public agency A*STAR fosters collaboration between research institutes, MNCs, SMEs, start-ups, as well as with other agencies, such as the Economic Development Board and SPRING Singapore. One-north was designed to bring people together and encourage serendipitous encounters between scientists and knowledge workers. The buildings are connected by sky bridges so people can walk from one research institute to another, there are also many spaces in common. Biopolis has an auditorium, lecture theatres, and meeting room. Spaces for collaboration have been designed to be shared by scientists and engineers in related disciplines, including the Zebra fish facility, bioreactor, electron microscopy, proteomics, MRI, histology, x-ray crystallography, DNA sequencing, lab supplies, media preparation, and glassware washing. Business schools such as ESSEC and INSEAD, corporate universities such as Unilever training center are located in Nepal Hill in the middle of one-north.

Creative

One-north proclaims itself as a place for knowledge workers and the creative class. On its promotional brochure, one-north is marketed as a place to "live-work-play-learn," which directly appeal to the creative class. One-north aims to attract the creative class by offering top amenities such as bars, clubs, and coffeehouses; creating "little bohemia" with heritage black-and-white colonial bungalows; offering cultural activities with the performance center; and offering one-north residents a great quality of life.

(Sources: Koh, 2006; Koh, & Tschang, 2005; Waldby, 2009; Wong & Bunnell, 2006; Wessner, 2009).

CONCLUSION

The fate of all innovation districts is unknown, and so the success of each depends on its urban leaders commitment to the project, as well as their ability to combine the right innovative processes during its construction. Innovation districts should not be seen as panacea for depressed cities, but rather as opportunities for urban leaders to experiment with innovative thinking in their cities. That being said, for small cities that have not achieved a sufficient innovative critical mass, attempting to develop innovation districts should be avoided. For cities to thrive in today's knowledge-economy, they must follow recipes for success that are significantly different from those that were followed in the mass-production economy. Indeed, in the past, urban leaders offered fiscal and economic incentives to encourage companies to relocate to their cities. This smokestack-chasing strategy adopted by cities resembled the cost leadership approach developed by Michael Porter, and therefore was a zero-sum game. Today, a number of cities within developed countries are adopting a competitive strategy, appealing to companies to relocate because of genuine interests to do so, such as access to talented, "creative" professionals, institutional supports, a high quality of life, an overall improved innovative capacity, and so on. Innovation districts such as 22@ Barcelona, Boston's Innovation District, and one-north Singapore are adopting this competitive strategy. In short, the cities that are implementing innovation districts aim to attract companies and individuals not through fiscal and economic incentives, but rather by providing what innovative companies, startups, entrepreneurs, and young professionals want. It is important to note that this competitive strategy can sometimes backfire. For instance, if City A adopts the same competitive strategies as city B, there is a chance that City A will become relatively less competitive than it was before. Indeed, the uniqueness of a place, which is what attracts the creative class in the first place, is lost as other cities attempt to replicate those same characteristics. The adaptability and absorptive capacities of innovation districts reinforce their complexity, and thus their ability to remain innovative in the long run.

In the framework developed in this toolkit, innovation districts are innovation ecosystems conceptualized around specific innovation models of which the mission is to accelerate the non-linear process of innovation. In Boston's Innovation district, the city's limited involvement in the project—as well as Thomas Menino's resigning from office in late 2013—have put the innovation district's development in jeopardy. Strong and smart leadership is required to transform a depressed urban district into a self-sustaining innovation district. Unfortunately for the United States, its institutional framework limits the public from direct involvement in such urban initiatives, as top-down, government strategies are often seen as inhibiting the free market. Strong city leadership and public involvement, however, are necessary for large, urban development or redevelopment projects that aim to build untraditional urban spaces such as innovation districts. Metropolitan areas must rethink and redefine their roles if they are to compete effectively in the knowledge-economy.

The success of the concept of innovation districts lies in their scalability and duplicability. Large cities can easily devote a district to an urban project that focuses on innovation. Indeed, the industrial restructuring that takes place in developed economies creates new opportunities for urban projects such as innovation districts. The presence of an innovation district in a city is a strong sign that its leaders are committed to innovation, and to improving the location's prosperity; moreover, the inhabitants of a city with an innovation district perceive the benefits of having it. After all, an innovation district is an initiative that is clearly visible to the city's residents, whereas a suburban technology park—government funded megaprojects designed as closed-systems, such as Paris-Saclay in France and Skolkovo in Russia—is not. The paradigm of technological parks built from an entirely top-down approach with strict zoning outside the city and closed systems are over. Urban projects must be open so that they can grow organically over the years and deliver on their promise to accelerate the process of innovation.

Barcelona is once again at the forefront of an urban revolution. The Barcelona model is still thriving, and 22@ Barcelona is being replicated all over the world, in cities as diverse as Boston (United States), Medellin (Colombia), and Montréal (Canada). Cities are adopting the innovation district model as a means of becoming—or remaining—competitive cities and knowledge hubs in the knowledge economy; however, the cities adopting these innovation-focused policies face rising inequalities and a number of urban challenges such as gentrification and the "disneyfication" of the city (Harvey, 2012). Among these challenges, gentrification is a reality and, as such, social policies must be smartly designed and implemented in order to limit it. Planned innovation districts have a greater chance of limiting gentrification than do spontaneous innovation districts because the former include social supports for the economically disadvantaged, such as public housing and educational facilities to retrain those whose skills do not match the needs of the new economy. Indeed, the rising gap between innovators and the rest of the population is growing. A dualism is emerging within innovation hubs and between the creative, innovative, and entrepreneurial haves and have-nots. Silicon Valley is not only the leading innovation hub in the world, but it is also the region with one of the largest homeless populations and homeless shelters—in the United States it is dubbed "the Jungle," (Gradydec, 2014). Urban leaders must find solutions to avoid creating increasingly unequal, dual cities (Castells, 1989). The uncertain future that disruptive technology creates must be dealt with, pragmatically, and, as such, those urban leaders who are the most pragmatic will also be the most successful.

REFERENCES

22@ Barcelona. (2011, December). Estado Actual. Retrieved from http://www.22barcelona.com/content/blogcategory/34/438/lang,es/

22@ Barcelona. (n.d). Barcelona, City Projects. Retrieved from http://w110.bcn.cat/fitxers/bcn-negocis/a22eng.175.pdf

Acitelli, T. (2011, December 13). South Boston to Get Hundred of Manhattan Apartments. *Curbed.* Retrieved from http://boston.curbed.com/archives/2011/12/south-boston-to-get-hundreds-of-manhattan-apartments.php

Allen, C. (2007). Of urban entrepreneurs or 24-hour party people? City-centre living in Manchester, England. *Environment and Planning A*, *39*(3), 666.

Allen, T. J. (1984*). Managing the flow of technology: Technology transfer and the dissemination of technological information within the R&D organization.* Cambridge, MA: MIT Press Books, 1.

Almirall, E., & Chesbrough, H. (2011). Open Innovation en el sector publico: el caso de urban labs. *Revista Económica de Cataluña*, (64), 100-109.

Anttiroiko, A. V. (2004). Editorial: Global competition of high-tech centres. *International journal of technology management. Vol 28. No 3/4/5/6*. Pp. 286-323.

Ashworth, G. J., & Voogd, H. (1990). *Selling the city: marketing approaches in public sector urban planning*. Belhaven Press.

Audretsch, D. B. (1998). Agglomeration and the location of innovative activity. *Oxford review of economic policy*, *14*(2), 18-29.

Audretsch, D. B., & Feldman, M. P. (1996). R&D spillovers and the geography of innovation and production. *The American economic review*, 630-640.

Audretsch, D. B., & Thurik, R. (Eds.). (1999). *Innovation, Industry Evolution and Employment*. Cambridge, UK: Cambridge University Press.

Auerswald, P. E., & Branscomb, L. M. (2003). Start-ups and spin-offs: Collective entrepreneurship between invention and innovation. *The Emergence of Entrepreneurship Policy: Governance, Start-Ups, and Growth in the US Knowledge Economy*, 61-91.

Babson. (n.d.). Babson Boston. Retrieved from http://www.babson.edu/admission/visiting-babson/boston/Pages/default.aspx

Ballester, P. (2013). Quartier d'artistes versus cluster numérique. Entre conflit foncier et production d'un nouvel espace créatif: le 22@ de Poblenou à Barcelone. *Territoire en mouvement Revue de géographie et aménagement. Territory in movement Journal of geography and planning*, (17-18), 73-90.

Barceló, M. (2005). Barcelona; 22@ Barcelona: A New District for the Creative Economy. Making Spaces for the Creative Economy.

Barceló, M., & Guillot, S. (2013). *Gestión de proyectos complejos*. Piramide.

Barceló, M., & Oliva, A. (2002). *La ciudad digital*. Pacto Industrial de la Región Metropolitana de Barcelona.

Barcelona Activa. (2012, November). Barcelona Smart City Tour. Retrieved from http://w42.bcn.cat/web/es/media-room/presentacions/index.jsp?componente=221-95513

Barcelona. (2000). *Modificación del PGM para la renovación de las zonas industriales del Poblenou - Districte d'Activitats 22@bcn*. Barcelona, Ayuntamiento de Barcelona. Retrieved from www.22barcelona.com/content/blogcategory/39/125/lang,ca.

Barcelona. (2012, June). El Plan 22@ Barcelona. Retrieved from http://www.22barcelona.com/documentacio/Dossier22@/Dossie

r%2022@Castellano_p.pdf

Battaglia, A., & Tremblay, D. G. (2012). 22@ and the Innovation District in Barcelona and Montreal: a process of clustering development between urban regeneration and economic competitiveness. *Urban Studies Research*, 2011.

Becattini, G. (1990). The Marshallian industrial district as a socio-economic notion. In Pyke, F., Becattini, G., Sengenberger, W. (Eds.), *Industrial districts and inter-firm cooperation in Italy*. (pp. 37-51). Geneva: International Institute for Labour Studies.

Begg, I. (Ed.). (2002). *Urban Competitiveness: Policies for dynamic cities*. Bristol: The policy press.

Belussi, F., & Sammarra, A. (Ed.). (2009). *Business networks in clusters and industrial districts: the governance of the global value chain*. London: Routledge.

Belussi, F., & Sedita, S. R. (2010). Localized and distance learning in industrial districts. Business Networks in Clusters and Industrial Districts. *The Governance of the Global Value Chain*, 24-51.

Bohlen, C. (1998, November 8). Facing Oblivion, Rust-Belt Giants Top Russian List of Vexing Crises. *The New York Times*.

Bontje, M., & Musterd, S. (2009). Creative industries, creative class and competitiveness: Expert opinions critically appraised. *Geoforum*, *40*(5), 843-852.

Boschma, R. A. (2005). Proximity and innovation: a critical assessment. *Regional studies*, *39*(1), 61-74.

Boschma, R.A., & Lambooy, J. G. (1998). Economic evolution and the adjustment of the spatial matrix of the regions. In: F. Boekema and J. van Dijk (Ed.), *Innovatie en bedrijf in de regio*. (pp. 121-138). Assen: Van Gorcum.

Boston Redevelopment Authority. (2010a, September 21). Seaport Square to Enhance City's Innovation District with New Innovation Center, 23-Acre Mixed-Use Sustainable Neighborhood. Retrieved from http://www.bostonredevelopmentauthority.org/news-calendar/news-updates/2010/09/21/seaport-square-to-enhance-city-e2-80-99s-innovatio

Boston Redevelopment Authority. (2010b). Development Plan for Planned Development Area No. 78 Seaport Square project. Boston Redevelopment Authority.

Boston Redevelopment Authority. (2013a, September 28). Ecodistricts. Retrieved from http://www.bostonredevelopmentauthority.org/planning/planning-initiatives/ecodistricts

Boston Redevelopment Authority. (2013b, November). Boston by the numbers Young Adults. Retrieved from http://www.bostonredevelopmentauthority.org/getattachment/bc819218-9b1d-4a3a-a94a-6a0a6822f3fa/

Boston Redevelopment Authority. (2013c, February 27). Boston by the numbers Colleges and Universities. Retrieved from http://www.bostonredevelopmentauthority.org/getattachment/3488e768-1dd4-4446-a557-3892bb0445c6/

Boston Redevelopment Authority. (2013d, December 27). BRA Disburses $100,000 to Fort Point Arts Community, Inc. Retrieved from http://www.bostonredevelopmentauthority.org/news-calendar/news-updates/2013/12/27/bra-awards-$100,000-grant-to-fort-point-arts-commu

Boston Redevelopment Authority. (2014a). Innovating Boston, one business at a time. Retrieved from http://www.bostonredevelopmentauthority.org/businessdev/initiatives/innovationboston/overview

Boston Redevelopment Authority. (2014b). Boston Marine Industrial Park (BMIP). Retrieved from http://www.bostonredevelopmentauthority.org/about-us/divisions/boston-marine-industrial-park/overview

Boston Redevelopment Authority. (2014c, January 30). New housing, retail, innovation space opens in Waterside Place on the South Boston Waterfront. Retrieved from http://www.bostonredevelopmentauthority.org/news-calendar/news-updates/2014/01/30/waterside-place-ribbon-cutting

Boston Redevelopment Authority. (2014d, February 4). Vertex Pharmaceuticals Opens on Fan Pier in Innovation District. Retrieved from http://www.bostonredevelopmentauthority.org/news-calendar/news-updates/2014/2/04/mayor-walsh-celebrates-vertex-opening-in-innovatio

Boston.com. (n.d.). Snapshots of Southie's transformation. *Boston.com.* Retrieved from http://www.boston.com/yourtown/boston/southboston/gallery/so uthie_evolution?pg=7

Bowles, J., & Gilles, D. (2012). *New Tech City*. Center for an Urban Future.

Branscomb, L. M. (2003, September). National innovation systems and US government policy. In *International Conference on Innovation in Energy Technologies." September* (Vol. 30).

Braun, E., & van Winden, W. (2014). Enhancing urban competitiveness through innovative growth clusters. In Ni, P., & Jie, Z. Q. (Ed.), *Urban Competitiveness and Innovation.* Cheltenham: Edward Elgar Publishing.

Breheny, M. (1996). Centrists, decentrists and compromisers: views on the future of urban form. *The compact city: A sustainable urban form*, 13-35.

Brynjolfsson, E., McAfee, A., Spence, M. (2014). New World Order Labor, Capital, and Ideas in the Power Law Economy. Foreign Affairs July/August 2014. Retrieved from: https://www.foreignaffairs.com/articles/united-states/2014-06-04/new-world-order

Burton, E., Jenks, M., & Williams, K. (Eds.). (2003). *The compact city: a sustainable urban form?*. London: Routledge.

Burton, E., Jenks, M., & Williams, K. (Eds.). (2013). *Achieving sustainable urban form*. London: Routledge.

Cairncross, F. (1997). *The Death of Distance*. Boston, MA: HBS Press.

Carayannis, E. G., & Campbell, D. F. (2009). 'Mode 3'and 'Quadruple Helix': toward a 21st century fractal innovation ecosystem. *International Journal of Technology Management*, *46*(3), 201-234.

Carlino, G. A. (2001). Knowledge spillovers: cities' role in the new economy. *Business Review Q*, *4*, 17-24.

Carlino, G. A., Chatterjee, S., & Hunt, R. M. (2007). Urban density and the rate of invention. *Journal of Urban Economics*, *61*(3), 389-419.

Carrillo, F. J. (2004). Capital cities: a taxonomy of capital accounts for knowledge cities. *Journal of Knowledge Management*, *8*(5), 28-46.

Castells, M. (1989). *The informational city: information technology, economic restructuring, and the urban-regional process*. Oxford: Blackwell.

Castells, M. (2011). *The rise of the network society: The information age: Economy, society, and culture* (Vol. 1). Hoboken: John Wiley & Sons.

Castells, M., & Hall, P. (1994). *Technopoles of the World: The Making of the 21st Century Industrial Complexes*. London: Routledge.

Castilla, E. J., Hwang, H., Granovetter, E., & Granovetter, M. (2000). Social networks in silicon valley. *The Silicon Valley edge: A habitat for innovation and entrepreneurship*, 218-247.

Charnock, G., & Ribera-Fumaz, R. (2011). A new space for knowledge and people? Henri Lefebvre, representations of space, and the production of 22@ Barcelona. *Environment and Planning-Part D*, *29*(4), 613.

Chatterji, A., Glaeser, E., & Kerr, W. (2013). Clusters of Entrepreneurship and Innovation. In *Innovation Policy and the Economy, Volume 14*. Chicago, IL: University of Chicago Press.

Chesbrough, H. W. (2003). *Open innovation: The new imperative for creating and profiting from technology*. Boston, MA: Harvard Business Press.

Chesbrough, H., & Crowther, A. K. (2006). Beyond high tech: early adopters of open innovation in other industries. *R&d Management*, *36*(3), 229-236.

Clark, G., Hutchins, M., Simmie, J., & Verdonk, H. (2004). *Competitive European cities: where do the core cities stand?*. London: Office of the Deputy Prime Minister.

Clark, J., Huang, H. I., & Walsh, J. P. (2010). A typology of 'innovation districts': what it means for regional resilience. *Cambridge Journal of Regions, Economy and Society*, *3*(1), 121-137.

Cortright, J. (2005). *The young and restless in a knowledge economy*. CEOs for Cities.

Da Cunha, I. V., & Selada, C. (2009). Creative urban regeneration: the case of innovation hubs. *International Journal of Innovation and Regional Development*, *1*(4), 371-386.

Duarte, F., & Sabaté, J. (2013). 22@ Barcelona: Creative Economy and Industrial Heritage–A Critical Perspective. *Theoretical and Empirical Researches in Urban Management*, *8*(2), 5-21.

Espelt-Lleonart, P. (2012). Building Barcelona's 22@ Innovation District: A technical Review. *The Journal of the Constructed Environment*. *2*(3), 113-134.

Etzkowitz, H. (2003). Innovation in innovation: The triple helix of university-industry-government relations. *Social science information*, *42*(3), 293-337.

Etzkowitz, H., & Leydesdorff, L. (2000). The dynamics of innovation: from National Systems and "Mode 2" to a Triple Helix of university–industry–government relations. *Research policy, 29*(2), 109-123.

Etzkowitz, H., Piqué, J. M., (2011). 22@ Barcelona: una ciudad del conocimiento más allá de los parques científicos y tecnológicos. *Revista Económica de Cataluña*, (64), 175-183.

Etzkowitz, H., Solé, F., & Piqué, J. M. (2010). The Creation of born Global Companies within the Science Cities: An approach from Triple Helix. *ENGEVISTA*, *9*(2).

European Commission. (1996). *DGs XIII and XVI RITTS and RIS Guidebook, Regional Actions for Innovation*. Brussels: EC.

European Commission. (2015). Youth employment. Retrieved from http://ec.europa.eu/social/main.jsp?catId=1036

European Union. (2010, September). Exhibition, Projecte Europa, EU Investments in Catalonia. Retrieved from http://ec.europa.eu/spain/Barcelona

Feld, B. (2012). *Startup communities: Building an entrepreneurial ecosystem in your city*. Hoboken, NJ: John Wiley & Sons.

Fischer, M. M. (2006). *Innovation, networks, and knowledge spillovers*. Berlin, Heidelberg: Springer.

Florida, R. (2002). *The rise of the creative class: and how it's transforming work, leisure, community and everyday life*. New York, NY: Basic books.

Florida, R. (2012, August 31). The Joys of Urban Tech. *The Wall Street Journal.*

Florida, R., & Kenney, M. (1993). The new age of capitalism: innovation-mediated production. *Futures*, *25*(6), 637-651.

Fujita, M., Krugman, P. R., & Venables, A. J. (2001). *The spatial economy: Cities, regions, and international trade*. Cambridge, MA: MIT press.

Gale International. (n.d). Songdo International Business District. Retrieved from http://www.galeintl.com/projects/songdo-ib/

Garriga, R., Sanchez, R., Solé Parellada, F. (2011). Los parques científicos y tecnológicos como plataforma empresarial global. *Revista Económica de Cataluña*, (64), 70-80.

Gibbons, J. F. (2000). The role of Stanford University: a Dean's reflections. *The Silicon Valley Edge, The Silicon Valley edge: A habitat for innovation and entrepreneurship* 200-217.

Gilly, J. P., & Torre, A. (2000). Proximity relations. Elements for an analytical framework. *Industrial Networks and Proximity*,

1-16.

Glaeser, E. L. (1998). Are cities dying?. *The Journal of Economic Perspectives*, 139-160.

Glaeser, E. L. (1999). Learning in cities. *Journal of urban Economics*, *46*(2), 254-277.

Glaeser, E. L. (2011). *Triumph of the city: How our greatest invention makes US richer, smarter, greener, healthier and happier*. New York, NY: Penguin Press.

Glaeser, E. L., & Maré, D. C. (1994). *Cities and skills* (No. w4728). National Bureau of Economic Research.

Glaeser, E. L., & Saiz, A. (2003). *The rise of the skilled city* (No. w10191). National Bureau of Economic Research.

Glaeser, E. L., Scheinkman, J., & Shleifer, A. (1995). Economic growth in a cross-section of cities. *Journal of monetary economics*, *36*(1), 117-143.

Gordon, P., & Richardson, H. W. (1997). Are compact cities a desirable planning goal?. *Journal of the American Planning Association*, *63*(1), 95-106.

Gradydec, B. (2014, December 4). Few Options for Homeless as San Jose Clears Camp. *The New York Times*. Retrieved from http://www.nytimes.com/2014/12/05/us/driven-from-silicon-valleys-jungle-homeless-face-limited-options.html

Granados, F. (2011). 22@ Barcelona y la gestion del talento innovador y emprendedor. *Revista Económica de Cataluña*, (64), 80-89.

Granovetter, M. (1973). The strength of weak ties. *American journal of sociology*, *78*(6), 1360-1380.

Groupe de Recherche Européen sur les Milieux Innovateurs. (1986). *Milieux innovateurs en Europe*. P. Aydalot (Ed.). Paris: GREMI.

Hall, P. (1988). *Cities of tomorrow*. Oxford: Basil Blackwell.

Hall, P. (1998). *Cities in civilization: culture, technology and urban order*. London: Weidenfield and Nicolson.

Hall, P. (2004). Creativity, culture, knowledge and the city. *Built Environment, 30*(3), 256-258.

Harvey, D. (2003). The right to the city. *International Journal of Urban and Regional Research, 27*(4), 939-941.

Harvey, D. (2012). *Rebel cities: from the right to the city to the urban revolution.* London: Verso Books.

HEC. (2015, March 24). Barometer of Entrepreneurship at HEC. Retrieved from http://www.hecalumni.fr/en/magazine/hec-life/hec-life/barometer-entrepreneurship-hec

Helft, M. (2011, May 17). For Buyers of Web Start-ups, Quest to Corral Young Talent. *The New York Times.*

Himanen, P. (2010). *The hacker ethic.* New York: Random House.

Howkins, J. (2002). *The creative economy: How people make money from ideas.* City of Westminster: Penguin UK.

Jacobs, J. (1961). *The death and life of great American cities.* New York, NY: Random House LLC.

Jacobs, J. (1969). *The economy of cities.* New York, NY: Vintage.

Jenks, M., & Burgess, R. (Ed.). (2000). *Compact cities: sustainable urban forms for developing countries.* London: Taylor & Francis.

Jeremy, R. (1995). *The end of work. The decline of the global labor force and the dawn of the post-market era.* New York: Putnam.

Kahneman, D., Krueger, A. B., Schkade, D. A., Schwarz, N., & Stone, A. A. (2004). A survey method for characterizing daily life experience: The day reconstruction method. *Science, 306*(5702), 1776-1780.

Keith, J. A. (2014, July 11). Innovation and Design Building Undergo Major Renovation. *Boston Magazine.* Retrieved from http://www.bostonmagazine.com/property/blog/2014/07/11/innovation-design-building-undergo-major-renovation/#gallery-1-2

Ketels, C. (2003, December). The Development of the cluster concept–present experiences and further developments. In *NRW conference on clusters, Duisburg, Germany* (Vol. 5).

Klinenberg, E. (2012). *Going solo: The extraordinary rise and surprising appeal of living alone*. City of Westminster: Penguin.

Knight, G. (1996). Born Global. *Wiley International Encyclopedia of Marketing*.

Knudsen, B., Florida, R., Gates, G., & Stolarick, K. (2007). Urban density, creativity and innovation. Working Paper of the Creative Class Group.

Koh, F. C., Koh, W. T., & Tschang, F. T. (2005). An analytical framework for science parks and technology districts with an application to Singapore. *Journal of Business Venturing*, *20*(2), 217-239.

Koh, W. T. (2006). Singapore's transition to innovation-based economic growth: infrastructure, institutions and government's role. *R&D Management*, *36*(2), 143-160.

Komninos, N. (2002). *Intelligent cities: innovation, knowledge systems, and digital spaces*. London: Taylor & Francis.

Kotkin, J., & DeVol, R. C. (2001). *Knowledge-value cities in the digital age*. Santa Monica, CA: Milken Institute.

Kresl, P. K. (2014). A development officer's guide to clusters. In Ni, P., & Jie, Z. Q. (Ed.), *Urban Competitiveness and Innovation*. Cheltenham: Edward Elgar Publishing.

Krier, L. (1977). The city within the city. *A+ U*, 69-152.

Krier, L. (1978). The reconstruction of the city. *The reconstruction of the European city: rational architecture, Archives d'Architecture Moderne, Brussels*.

Krier, L. (1984). Urban components. *Architectural Design*, *54*(7/8), 43.

Landry, C. (2008). *The creative city: A toolkit for urban innovators*. London: Earthscan.

Lanier, J. (2014). *Who owns the future?*. New York: Simon and

Schuster.

Le Corbusier. (1946). *Manière de penser l'urbanisme: urbanisme des CIAM (Vol. 1)*. Éditions de l'architecture d'aujourd'hui.

Leon, N. (2008). Attract and connect: The 22@ Barcelona innovation district and the internationalization of Barcelona business. *Innovation: Management, Policy & Practice*, *10*(2-3), 235-246.

Lever, W. F. (2002). The knowledge base and the competitive city. In Begg, I., (Ed.), *Urban Competitiveness: Policies for dynamic cities.* (pp. 11-31). Bristol: The Policy Press.

Ley, D. (2003). Artists, aestheticisation and the field of gentrification. *Urban studies*, *40*(12), 2527-2544.

Leydesdorff, L., & Etzkowitz, H. (1996). Emergence of a Triple Helix of university-industry-government relations. *Science and public policy*, *23*(5), 279-286.

Leydesdorff, L., & Etzkowitz, H. (1998). The triple helix as a model for innovation studies. *Science and public policy*, *25*(3), 195-203.

Leydesdorff, L., & Meyer, M. (2008). The triple helix model and the knowledge-based economy. *Scientometrics*, forthcoming.

López, A., Romani, A., Sagarra, R., Piqué, J. H. (2011). 22@Barcelona: exportando el modelo. *Revista Económica de Cataluña*, (64), 70-79.

Mahroum, S. (2000). Highly skilled globetrotters: mapping the international migration of human capital. *R&D Management*, *30*(1), 23-32.

Majó, A. (2011). 22@ Urban labs el ejemplo de Barcelona. *Revista Económica de Cataluña*, (64), 100-109

Malecki, E. J. (2002). Hard and soft networks for urban competitiveness. *Urban Studies*, *39*(5-6), 929-945.

Manski, C. F. (2000). Economic Analysis of Social Interactions. *The Journal of Economic Perspectives*, *14*(3), 115-136.

Markantoni, M., Koster, S. & Strijker D. (2012). Side activity Entrepreneur: Lifestyle or Economic Oriented. In Karlsson, J. and R., Stough (Ed.), *Agglomeration, Clusters and Entrepreneurship: Studies in Regional Economic Development*. Cheltenham: Edward Elgar Publishing.

Marshall, A. (1920). Principles of economics: an introductory volume.

Martin, R., & Sunley, P. (2003). Deconstructing clusters: chaotic concept or policy panacea?. *Journal of economic geography*, *3*(1), 5-35.

Mazzarol, T., Volery, T., Doss, N., & Thein, V. (1999). Factors influencing small business start-ups: a comparison with previous research. *International Journal of Entrepreneurial Behaviour & Research*, *5*(2), 48-63.

McDougall, P. P., & Oviatt, B. M. (2003). Some fundamental issues in international entrepreneurship. *Entrepreneurship Theory & Practice*, *18*, 27.

Miller, R. E., & Cote, M. (1987). *Growing the next Silicon Valley: A guide for successful regional planning*. Free Press.

Mobile World Capital. **(2012, March 28).** Barcelona creates a "free trade zone" for mobile technology focused companies. Retrieved from http://mobileworldcapital.com/en/article/33

Molas, O., & Sabata, M. P. (2011). 22@: 10 años de transformación económica. *Revista Económica de Cataluña*, (64), 13-21.

Mommaas, H. (2004). Cultural clusters and the post-industrial city: towards the remapping of urban cultural policy. *Urban studies*, *41*(3), 507-532.

Montgomery, C. (2013). *Happy city: transforming our lives through urban design*. London: Macmillan.

Moretti, E. (2012). *The new geography of jobs*. Boston, MA: Houghton Mifflin Harcourt.

Morgan, K. (2004). The exaggerated death of geography: learning, proximity and territorial innovation systems. *Journal of economic geography*, *4*(1), 3-21.

Mould, O. (2014). Mediating the city: The role of planned Media cities in the geographies of creative industry activity. *Hub Cities in the Knowledge Economy: Seaports, Airports, Brainports*. Farnham: Ashgate Publishing, Ltd.

Mumford, L. (1961). *The city in history: its origins, its transformations, and its prospects*. San Diego, CA: Harcourt, Brace & World, Inc.

Munroe, T. (2010, July 3). Incubators Fertile Ground for Job Creation. *Contra Costa Times*.

Neff, J. (2010). Is Digital Revolution Driving Decline in US Car Culture. *Advertising Age*, *31*.

OECD. (1998). *University Research in Transition*. OECD, Paris.

Oldenburg, R. (1989). *The great good place: Cafés, coffee shops, community centers, beauty parlors, general stores, bars, hangouts, and how they get you through the day*. New York, NY: Paragon House.

Oliva, A. (2003). 22@ BCN Activities District. *Aula Barcelona Management Booklets*, *15*.

Oviatt, B. M., McDougall, P. P., & Loper, M. (1995). Global start-ups: Entrepreneurs on a worldwide stage [and executive commentary]. *The Academy of Management Executive (1993-2005)*, 30-44.

Pareja-Eastway, M. (2011). Ciudades Creativas, un nuevo paradigmo para las agendas locales?. *Revista Económica de Cataluña*, (64), 130-140.

Phillimore, J., & Joseph, R. (2003). Science parks: A triumph of hype over experience. *The international handbook on innovation*, 750-757.

Pinch, S., Henry, N., Jenkins, M., & Tallman, S. (2003). From 'industrial districts' to 'knowledge clusters': a model of knowledge dissemination and competitive advantage in industrial agglomerations. *Journal of Economic Geography*, *3*(4), 373-388.

Pine, B. J., & Gilmore, J. H. (1998). Welcome to the experience economy. *Harvard business review*, (*76)*, 97-105.

Polanyi, M. (1966). The logic of tacit inference. *Philosophy*, *41*(155), 1-18.

Porter, L., & Barber, A. (2007). Planning the cultural quarter in Birmingham's Eastside. *European planning studies*, *15*(10), 1327-1348.

Porter, M. E. (1990). The Competitive Advantage of Nations. *Harvard Business Review*, *68*(2), 73-93.

Porter, M. E. (2008). *On Competition*. Boston, MA: Harvard Business Press.

Porter, M. E. (2011). *Competitive advantage of nations: creating and sustaining superior performance*. New York, NY: Simon and Schuster.

Porter, M. E., Ketels, C., Habiby, A., & Zipper, D. (2008). New York City: Bloomberg's Strategy for Economic Development. *Harvard Business School*.

Quintas, P., Wield, D., & Massey, D. (1992). Academic-industry links and innovation: questioning the science park model. *Technovation*, *12*(3), 161-175.

Ricken, B., & Malcotsis, G. (2011). *The Competitive Advantage of Regions and Nations: Technology Transfer Through Foreign Direct Investment*. Farnham: Gower Publishing.

Roberts, E. B., & Eesley, C. E. (2011). *Entrepreneurial impact: The role of MIT*. Boston, MA: Now Publishers.

Rosen, S. (1981). The economics of superstars. *The American economic review*, 71 (5). pp. 845-858.

Ross, C. (2010, September 1). New era docks on the waterfront. *The Boston Globe*. Retrieved from http://www.boston.com/business/articles/2010/09/01/60m_libert y_wharf_complex_showcases_public_open_spaces/

Rotman, D. (2015, June 6). Who Will Own the Robots?. MIT Technology Review. Retrieved from: http://www.technologyreview.com/featuredstory/538401/who-will-own-the-robots/

Sabaté, J., & Tironi, M. (2008). Rankings, creatividad y urbanismo. *EURE (Santiago), 34*(102), 5-23.

Sabel, C., & Piore, M. (1984). *The second industrial divide.* New York, NY: Basic Book.

Savitch, H. V. (1988). *Post-industrial cities.* Princeton, NJ: Princeton University Press.

Saxenian, A. (1994). *Regional advantage: Culture and competition in Silicon Valley and Route 128.* Boston, MA: Harvard University.

Saxenian, A. (2006). *The new argonauts: Regional advantage in a global economy.* Boston, MA: Harvard University Press.

Schumpeter, J. (2013). *Capitalism, socialism and democracy.* London: Routledge.

Scott, A. J. (1997). The cultural economy of cities. *International journal of urban and regional research, 21*(2), 323-339.

Sharma, P. (2012). Innovation Districts: A Look at Communities Spurring Economic Development Through Collaboration. *New Jersey Future.*

Siegel, D. S., Westhead, P., & Wright, M. (2003). Assessing the impact of university science parks on research productivity: exploratory firm-level evidence from the United Kingdom. *International Journal of Industrial Organization, 21*(9), 1357-1369.

Simmie, J. (2004). Innovation clusters and competitive cities in the UK and Europe. In Boddy, M., & Parkinson, M. (Ed.), *City matters: Competitiveness, cohesion and urban governance.* (pp.171-196). Bristol: Policy Press.

Simmie, J. (Ed.). (2013). *Innovative cities.* London: Routledge.

Smith, N. (1996). *The new urban frontier: Gentrification and the revanchist city.* Psychology Press.

Smith, N. (2002). New globalism, new urbanism: gentrification as global urban strategy. *Antipode, 34*(3), 427-450.

South Boston Waterfront Sustainable Transportation Plan. (2014). Existing Conditions Report. Retrieved from http://www.sbwaterfrontmobility.org/

Speck, J. (2013). *Walkable city: How downtown can save America, one step at a time*. London: Macmillan.

Stimson, R. J., Stough, R. R., & Roberts, B. H. (2006). *Regional economic development*. Berlin, Heidelberg: Springer.

Storper, M. (2013). *Keys to the city: how economics, institutions, social interaction, and politics shape development*. Princeton, NJ: Princeton University Press.

Suire, R., & Vicente, J. (2009). Why do some places succeed when others decline? A social interaction model of cluster viability. *Journal of Economic Geography*, *9*(3), 381-404.

Tallman, S., Jenkins, M., Henry, N., & Pinch, S. (2004). Knowledge, clusters, and competitive advantage. *Academy of management review*, *29*(2), 258-271.

Trullén, J. (2001). El projecte Barcelona. Ciutat del coneixement desde l'economia. *Barcelona, metrópolis mediterrània*.

Trullén, J. (2011). El proyecto Barcelona Ciudad del Conocimiento y el 22@Barcelona. *Revista Económica de Cataluña*, (64), 22-30.

Trullén, J., Lladós, J., & Boix R. (2002). Economía del conocimiento, ciudad y competitividad. *Investigaciones regionales*, (1), 139-161.

Van Winden, W., De Carvalho, L., van Tuijl, E., van Haaren, J., & van den Berg, L. (2013). *Creating knowledge locations in cities: Innovation and integration challenges*. London: Routledge.

Vicente, J., Dalla Pria, Y., & Suire, R. (2007). The ambivalent role of mimetic behaviors in proximity dynamics: evidences on the French 'Silicon Sentier.' In Surin, J., & Moreno, R. (Ed.), *Knowledge externalities, innovation clusters and regional development*. (pp. 61-91). Cheltenham: Edward Elgar Publishing.

Wadhwa, V., Freeman, R., & Rissing, B. (2010). Education and tech entrepreneurship. *innovations*, *5*(2), 141-153.

Waldby, C. (2009). Singapore Biopolis: bare life in the city-state. *East Asian Science, Technology and Society*, *3*(2-3), 367-383.

Wessner, C. W. (Ed.). (2009). *Understanding Research, Science and Technology Parks: Global Best Practice: Report of a Symposium*. National Academies Press.

Wieckowski, A. (2010). Back to the City. *Harvard Business Review*, *88*(5), 23-25.

Wong, K. W., & Bunnell, T. (2006). New economy' discourse and spaces in Singapore: a case study of one-north. *Environment and Planning A, 38*(1) 69-83.

World Bank. (1992). Export Processing Zone. Industry and Development Division.

Wood, P., Simmie, J., & Sennett, J. (2002). Innovation and clustering in the London metropolitan region. In Begg, I., (Ed.), *Urban Competitiveness: Policies for dynamic cities*. (pp. 161-190). Bristol: The Policy Press.

Worpole, K., & Greenhalgh, L. (1999). *The Richness of Cities: Urban Policy in a New Landscape*. London: Routledge.

Youtie, J., & Shapira, P. (2008). Building an innovation hub: A case study of the transformation of university roles in regional technological and economic development. *Research policy*, *37*(8), 1188-1204.

Zukin, S. (1989). *Loft living: culture and capital in urban change*. Rutgers, NJ: Rutgers University Press.